CAMBRIDGE LIBRARY COLLECTION

Books of enduring scholarly value

Classics

From the Renaissance to the nineteenth century, Latin and Greek were compulsory subjects in almost all European universities, and most early modern scholars published their research and conducted international correspondence in Latin. Latin had continued in use in Western Europe long after the fall of the Roman empire as the lingua franca of the educated classes and of law, diplomacy, religion and university teaching. The flight of Greek scholars to the West after the fall of Constantinople in 1453 gave impetus to the study of ancient Greek literature and the Greek New Testament. Eventually, just as nineteenth-century reforms of university curricula were beginning to erode this ascendancy, developments in textual criticism and linguistic analysis, and new ways of studying ancient societies, especially archaeology, led to renewed enthusiasm for the Classics. This collection offers works of criticism, interpretation and synthesis by the outstanding scholars of the nineteenth century.

An Enquiry into the Ancient Routes between Italy and Gaul

The controversy over the route taken by Hannibal, the Carthaginian army and his famous elephants in their crossing of the Alps to attack Rome in 218 BCE began within fifty years of the event and has continued for many centuries. A particular scholarly dispute emerged in the 1850s between Robert Ellis (1819/20–85) and William John Law (1786–1869), and was fought in the pages of the *Journal of Classical and Sacred Philology* and in books. Ellis, a classical scholar, had surveyed the Alpine passes in 1852 and again in 1853, when he published his *Treatise on Hannibal's Passage of the Alps* (also reissued in this series), claiming that the Little Mount Cenis route was the one used. Law responded immediately in the *Journal*, and later published his own theory, to which Ellis riposted in 1867 with this work. Modern scholarship doubts, however, that either man was right.

Cambridge University Press has long been a pioneer in the reissuing of out-of-print titles from its own backlist, producing digital reprints of books that are still sought after by scholars and students but could not be reprinted economically using traditional technology. The Cambridge Library Collection extends this activity to a wider range of books which are still of importance to researchers and professionals, either for the source material they contain, or as landmarks in the history of their academic discipline.

Drawing from the world-renowned collections in the Cambridge University Library and other partner libraries, and guided by the advice of experts in each subject area, Cambridge University Press is using state-of-the-art scanning machines in its own Printing House to capture the content of each book selected for inclusion. The files are processed to give a consistently clear, crisp image, and the books finished to the high quality standard for which the Press is recognised around the world. The latest print-on-demand technology ensures that the books will remain available indefinitely, and that orders for single or multiple copies can quickly be supplied.

The Cambridge Library Collection brings back to life books of enduring scholarly value (including out-of-copyright works originally issued by other publishers) across a wide range of disciplines in the humanities and social sciences and in science and technology.

An Enquiry into the Ancient Routes between Italy and Gaul

With an Examination of the Theory of Hannibal's Passage of the Alps by the Little St Bernard

Robert Ellis

CAMBRIDGE
UNIVERSITY PRESS

CAMBRIDGE
UNIVERSITY PRESS

University Printing House, Cambridge, CB2 8BS, United Kingdom

Cambridge University Press is part of the University of Cambridge.
It furthers the University's mission by disseminating knowledge in the pursuit of
education, learning and research at the highest international levels of excellence.

www.cambridge.org
Information on this title: www.cambridge.org/9781108075763

© in this compilation Cambridge University Press 2014

This edition first published 1867
This digitally printed version 2014

ISBN 978-1-108-07576-3 Paperback

This book reproduces the text of the original edition. The content and language reflect
the beliefs, practices and terminology of their time, and have not been updated.

Cambridge University Press wishes to make clear that the book, unless originally published
by Cambridge, is not being republished by, in association or collaboration with,
or with the endorsement or approval of, the original publisher or its successors in title.

The original edition of this book contains a number of colour plates,
which have been reproduced in black and white. Colour versions of these
images can be found online at www.cambridge.org/9781108075763

AN ENQUIRY, &c.

AN ENQUIRY

INTO THE

ANCIENT ROUTES BETWEEN ITALY AND GAUL;

WITH AN EXAMINATION OF THE THEORY

OF

HANNIBAL'S PASSAGE OF THE ALPS

BY THE LITTLE ST. BERNARD.

BY

ROBERT ELLIS, B.D.,

FELLOW OF ST. JOHN'S COLLEGE, CAMBRIDGE.

Διὸ καὶ παρὰ βραχὺ μὲν ἢ καὶ ἀγνοεῖν ἢ καὶ ψευδοδοξεῖν, δεδόσθω
συγγνώμη· τὸ δ' ὑπεραῖρον ἀθετείσθω, κατά γε τὴν ἐμὴν δόξαν.

POLYBIUS, xvi. 12.

CAMBRIDGE:

DEIGHTON, BELL, & CO., TRINITY STREET;
LONDON: BELL AND DALDY.

1867.

Cambridge:

PRINTED BY JONATHAN PALMER, JESUS LANE.

THE Map of the Cottian and Maritime Alps is to be placed at the beginning of the book, and the Plan of the Mont Cenis at the end.

The modern distances in the book are derived from the Map called *La France en kilomètres*, and from the *Itinerario degli Stati Sardi*. Strabo is cited, after the usual manner, according to the paging of Casaubon.

A degree is divided (neglecting fractions) into 45 Piedmontese miles, 60 Italian miles, 69 English miles, 75 (ancient) Roman miles, and 111 kilomètres. A Roman mile of 8 stadia is consequently very nearly equal to $\frac{2}{3}$ of a Piedmontese mile, $\frac{4}{5}$ of an Italian mile, $\frac{11}{12}$ of an English mile, and $\frac{3}{2}$ kilomètres.

CONTENTS.

CHAPTER VII.

CHAPTER VIII.

APPENDIX.

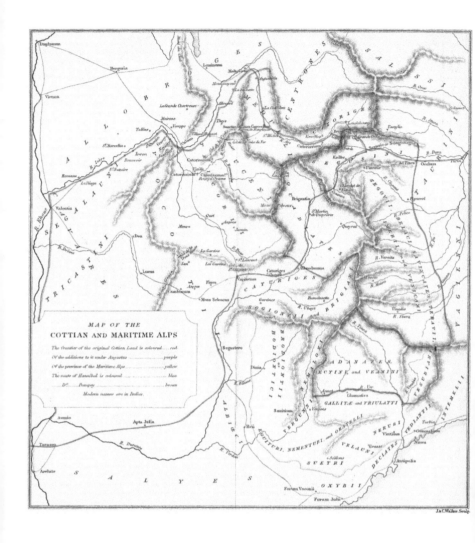

The material originally positioned here is too large for reproduction in this reissue. A PDF can be downloaded from the web address given on page iv of this book, by clicking on 'Resources Available'.

AN ENQUIRY, &c.

CHAPTER I.

INTRODUCTION—EXAMINATION OF THE STRONG POINT OF THE BERNARDINE THEORY—PROOF THAT THE PLAINS AT THE FOOT OF HANNIBAL'S ALPS WERE OCCUPIED BY THE TAURINI.

It is not my intention, in this present work, to go again over the same ground as I occupied in my Treatise on Hannibal's Passage of the Alps, with the exception of such points as I noticed there in my last chapter, but without doing them justice. Of the agreement of the route of the Mont Cenis with the description of Polybius entirely, and with that of Livy in all trustworthy points, I shall therefore say as little as possible; as it will be my aim to prove now, by another line of argument, that Hannibal crossed the Little Mont Cenis. The course which I shall pursue is this. I shall first try to narrow the question by disposing of the theory of the Little St. Bernard, while that of the Great St. Bernard will follow. And here I shall have to consider the work on the credit of which the former theory mainly rests in England, the Dissertation of Messrs. Wickham and Cramer. My citations and references will be taken from the second edition of that work, published nine years after the first, and which may thus be expected

B

to contain the matured arguments and opinions of its writers, and to exhibit the manner in which they consider that their case may be best supported. To this dissertation have been lately added two ingenious volumes on the 'Alps of Hannibal' by my old antagonist, Mr. Law.

My first chapter will be mainly devoted to the proof of one point; namely, that Hannibal traversed a pass leading through the country of the Taurini. If this point be clearly proved, as I trust will be done, it is decisive against the Bernardine theory; and no further arguments would be required on the subject, although I have thought it as well to devote another chapter to its consideration. The fact that Hannibal traversed a pass leading through the country of the Taurini being thus settled, the only question which remains to be determined is, by which of the two passes, the Mont Genèvre or the Mont Cenis, did he cross the Alps? Before entering upon this question, I shall have to prepare the way by two chapters on the Cottian Land and other points of geography, proving my map, as I may say, before I advance farther. I shall then consider the Cottian pass of Artemidorus, and shew the probable identity, merely from the consideration of distance, both of this pass and that of Hannibal, with the Mont Cenis, and not with the Mont Genèvre. I next come to the pass of Pompey, which, like that of Hannibal, would have been a Cottian pass; so that, of the two Cottian passes, the Mont Cenis and the Mont Genèvre, one would have been crossed by Pompey and the other by Hannibal; the shorter and more convenient route of the two, the Mont Genèvre, being necessarily that of Pompey. This completes the proof that Hannibal

crossed the Mont Cenis. My two concluding chapters
relate to other ancient routes. In one I examine the
routes of Cæsar and Plancus, and in the other endeavour to identify two routes, given in the Peutingerian Table, through the Cottian Alps.

I commence my argument by examining the *strong*
point of the Bernardine theory.

What is supposed to be this strong point is derived
from the following passage in Polybius (III. 56) :

"Finally, having accomplished his whole march from
New Carthage in five months, and his passage of the Alps
in fifteen days, Hannibal descended boldly into the plains of
the Po and the Insubrian country (κατῆρε τολμηρῶς εἰς τὰ
περὶ τὸν Πάδον πεδία, καὶ τὸ τῶν Ἰσόμβρων ἔθνος).

It is inferred from these words that the Insubres
occupied the plains at the foot of Hannibal's Alps,
and that Hannibal must therefore have crossed the
Little (or Great) St. Bernard, and not either of the
Cottian passes, the Mont Genèvre or Mont Cenis,
which would require that the plains at the foot of
Hannibal's Alps should be occupied by the Taurini.

Against this inference and conclusion I shall
endeavour to prove four points :

1. If the Insubres occupied the plains at the foot
of Hannibal's Alps, the Bernardine theory falls to the
ground.

2. The words relied on are not sufficient to prove
that those plains were occupied by the Insubres.

3. The words refer to Hannibal's march to the
Ticinus, where he was encountered by Scipio.

4. The plains of the Taurini are twice placed by
Polybius at the foot of Hannibal's Alps, and the
same opinion was universally held by the ancients;

so that Hannibal must of necessity have crossed the Cottian Alps.

These points I shall now take in their order.

1. The plains at the foot of the Bernardine Alps were occupied by the Libui, and not by the Insubres. This fact, well known to all who are acquainted with ancient geography, is noticed by Livy (xxi. 38), when he says that the passes of the Little and Great St. Bernard would have brought Hannibal down, "non in Taurinos, sed per Salassos montanos ad Libuos Gallos." Ptolemy, again, who gives Ivrea to the Salassi, assigns to the Libui the towns of Vercelli on the Sesia, and Lomello on the Agogna, while he gives to the Insubres those of Milan, Como, Novara (founded by the Vertacomacori), and Pavia (founded by the Lævi and Marici). Polybius gives them Milan and Acerræ.[1] The boundary between the Insubres and the Libui would consequently have been the Agogna, while to the west we may consider, with Cluverius, that the Libui were divided from the Taurini by the Orco, which joins the Po near Chivasso. The territory of the Libui, with whom the Lævi are usually associated, would thus have lain between the Orco and the Agogna, the Alps and the Po, and have been intersected by the Dora Baltea and the Sesia. If, then, the Insubres lived at the foot of Hannibal's Alps, Hannibal did not cross the Little or Great St. Bernard.

This simple argument Messrs Wickham and Cramer try to meet in two ways inconsistent with each

---

[1] The eastern boundary of the Insubres is fixed by Polybius (ii. 32) at the Clusius (*Chiese*). In this direction they seem afterwards to have lost territory to the Cenomani, who were usually allies of the Romans in their wars against the Boii and Insubres. See Spruner's *Ancient Atlas*.

other. By one, the Libui are shifted into the country of the Taurini, and the Insubres moved up to the Orco : by the other, the Libui are allowed to remain in their proper place, but converted into Insubres.

In the first case, Messrs. W. and C. rely on a passage in Polybius (II. 17), where he speaks of the Gauls expelling the Etruscans from the plains of the Po, and settling there themselves.   Here Messrs. W. and C. observe (p. 37):

" Polybius mentions the Laii and Lebecii (Lævi and Libui of the Romans) as being settled near the sources of the Po, after whom come the Insubres, that is, at the spot where the river, instead of running from S. to N., turns to the eastward, which is at Chivasso."

I need do no more than quote these words, as it must be unnecessary for me to prove to any one that the Libui and Lævi never expelled the Etruscans from the plains of Turin, and took possession of them. What is to become of the Taurini ? I will merely point out how inconsistent Messrs. W. and C. are in making the Libui and Lævi extend no further to the east than Chivasso in p. 37, and in assigning to the same Libui and Lævi, in p. 32, the towns of Vercelli, Lomello, and Pavia.

The argument by which the Libui are made Insubres is derived from Ptolemy :

" The Libui are reckoned" (*i. e.* included) " by Ptolemy under the Insubres" (p. 147).

This rests upon Ptolemy's words (III. 1): Λιβικῶν ὑπὸ τοὺς Ἰνσούβρους.   Mere citation is again quite sufficient for me ; for no one can expect me to try to prove that ὑπό signifies here "lying under or contiguous to," and has nothing to do with inclusion

or subordination.   But I may point out how partially
Messrs. W. and C. apply their erroneous interpretation
of ὑπό.   In the same place (ed. Tauchnitz, p. 146)
where the Libui are placed by Ptolemy 'under' the
Insubres, the Taurini are placed 'under' the Salassi,
and the Salassi 'under' the Insubres.   If then the
Libui were Insubres, so also were the Salassi and
Taurini.   And, indeed, Messrs. W. and C. tell us in
a note (p. 120) that Ptolemy ranks the Salassi under
the Insubres as well as the Libicii; but of the Taurini
being Insubrian also we never hear anything.

The Libui are thus clearly distinguished from the
Insubres in the preceding citations from Ptolemy and
Polybius.   The Lævi and Libui, mentioned by Livy
(xxxiii. 37) in the year 196 B.C., could not, again,
have been Insubrian, for their territory was ravaged
by the allies of the Insubres, the Boii; and it is
reasonable to suppose that the Libui were included
among the Barbarians who are mentioned by Polybius
(iii. 60) as submitting to Hannibal after the fall of
Turin.

I have now but to add Mr. Law's solution of the
difficulty (vol. i. p. 305), which I shall pass without
comment:

"Who can resist the probability, that minor tribes who
had first settled in that plain, and were probably still its
occupants in name, had become subordinate to their more
powerful neighbour?   Is it any stretch of imagination, to
believe that Insubrian chieftains and an Insubrian force
should be on the banks of the Doria to welcome the approach
of their illustrious ally?"

2. The second point which I have to prove is:
That the words, "he descended boldly (from the
foot of the Alps) into the plains of the Po and the

Insubrian country," are insufficient to prove that the Insubres lay at the foot of the Alps of Hannibal.

In the first place it may be urged, that "the plains of the Po and the Insubrian country" do not necessarily mean nothing more than "the Insubrian country" only. *Tὰ περὶ τὸν Πάδον πεδία καὶ τὸ τῶν Ἰσόμβρων ἔθνος*, must not be assumed as = *ἡ τῶν Ἰσόμβρων χώρα*. Hannibal may, as far as these words of Polybius are concerned, have been in the plains of the Po before he reached the Insubrian country; and in point of fact, as will be hereafter shewn, the country of the Insubres was the last, not the first part of the plains which Hannibal reached on this march. It was not his starting-point in the plains, but his goal, and is mentioned on that account.

But again: even if Polybius had written, as he has not, *κατῆρε τολμηρῶς εἰς τὴν τῶν Ἰσόμβρων χώραν*, yet this would not prove the Insubrian hypothesis. Appian writes of Cæsar (*Bell. Civ.* II. 32): *τὰ ὄρη τὰ Ἄλπεια διελθὼν σὺν πεντακισχιλίοις πεζοῖς καὶ ἱππεῦσι τριακοσίοις, κατέβαινεν ἐπὶ Ῥαβέννης*. Does this descent upon Ravenna prove beyond controversy that Ravenna lies at the foot of the Alps? Or what inconsistency would there be in saying: "Hannibal, having crossed the Cottian Alps, descended boldly to the Milanese?" especially when we remember that the Milanese, the country of his promised allies, the Insubres, was his mark from the time he started from Carthagena, and might naturally be named for that reason, just as Appian names Ravenna in Cæsar's case.

I may also mention that the words, *κατῆρε τολμηρῶς*, would be more applicable to a march where there was hostility to be expected, than to a peaceful halt in a friendly country.

3. The third point for demonstration is:

The words, κατῆρε τολμηρῶς κ. τ. λ., refer to Hannibal's march to the Ticinus, where he was encountered by Scipio.

The elucidation of this point will require a complete examination of the narrative of Polybius. Now this narrative, up to the date of the battle of the Ticinus, is devoted to the operations of two armies; of the army of the Carthaginians under Hannibal, and of the army of the Romans under Scipio. Hannibal is first described as starting from Carthagena, and crossing the Ebro and the Pyrenees; and Scipio then (c. 41) as sailing from Pisa to the Massiliotic mouth of the Rhone, and as hearing of Hannibal's passage of the Pyrenees. He next hears (*ib.*) of Hannibal's arrival on the Rhone (nearly four days' march from its mouth), and sends out a body of horse in that direction. Hannibal now passes the Rhone, and, having heard of the landing of the Romans, detaches a body of five hundred Numidian horse to observe their movements (c. 44). In c. 45 the two bodies of cavalry meet; the Romans have the advantage; and both detachments return to their main armies. Having brought his elephants, which had been left behind, over the Rhone, Hannibal next starts up that river (c. 47); and Scipio, coming to where Hannibal had crossed the Rhone, and finding him gone to pass the Alps, sent his brother into Spain, and returned himself into Italy, so as to get before Hannibal to the passage of the Alps: τὸν μὲν ἀδελφὸν ἐξέπεμπεν ἐπὶ τὰς ἐν Ἰβηρίᾳ πράξεις· αὐτὸς δὲ, πάλιν ὑποστρέψας εἰς Ἰταλίαν ἐποιεῖτο τὸν πλοῦν, σπεύδων καταταχῆσαι τοὺς ὑπεναντίους διὰ Τυρρηνίας πρὸς τὴν τῶν Ἄλπεων ὑπερβολήν (c. 49). This intention of Scipio's to gain the Alpine pass from the Italian side, before Hannibal could get there, should be borne in mind. He was, however, as we shall see, unable to carry it out completely, for he had advanced no farther than the Ticinus when he was met by Hannibal, who had arrived at the commencement of the Italian plain a considerable time before.

The following would be the nearly synchronistic movements of the two generals, from the time of their action on the Rhone up to the date of the battle of the Ticinus.

{ Hannibal marches to the 'Island'.
{ Scipio returns to the coast.

{ Hannibal marches to the Gallic foot of the Alps.
{ Scipio sails back to Pisa.

{ Hannibal crosses the Alps.
{ Scipio crosses the Apennines.

{ Hannibal descends into the plains of the Po from the Alps.
{ Scipio descends into the plains of the Po from the Apennines.

{ Hannibal arrives on the Ticinus (the country of the Insu-
{ bres), and is there opposed by Scipio.

No one, I think, will dispute any of these points. Whatever pass of the Alps Hannibal may have crossed, yet it must at least be universally acknowledged, that when he marched down to the Ticinus after the siege of Turin to meet the Romans, he then descended boldly to the country of the Insubres; and if his arrival at that country is mentioned by an historian as coinciding in point of time with his being opposed by Scipio, there ought not to remain any doubt that it was Hannibal's march to the Ticinus which is described as his descent to the Insubrian country.

Now this, it will be seen, is what is done by

Polybius. After mentioning (c. 49) Scipio's voyage back to Pisa, and his intention of gaining the pass of the Alps from the Italian side before Hannibal could get there, he says nothing more of the Roman general till c. 56. From c. 49 to the beginning of c. 56 Hannibal's march from the passage of the Rhone, across the Alps, to the commencement of the Italian plain, is described at length, and the 56th chapter then runs on thus to its end:

Finally (Hannibal), having accomplished his whole march from New Carthage in five months,

and his passage of the Alps in fifteen days,

descended boldly into the plains of the Po *and the country of the Insubres :*

having saved of his Libyan forces 12000 men, and of his Iberians 8000 ; but of his cavalry not more than 6000 in all, as he himself states on the column at Lacinium containing the account of his numbers.

And at the same time (κατὰ δὲ τοὺς αὐτοὺς καιρούς), as I said previously, Publius (Scipio) having left his forces (on the Rhone) with his brother Cnæus, and having exhorted him to attend to the affairs of Spain, and to make war vigorously upon Hasdrubal, sailed himself with a few men to Pisa. And having marched through Etruria, and having received from the prætors the troops which were making war on the Boii and holding their country, he came to the plains of the Po, and, *having encamped, he opposed the enemy (the Carthaginians), being bent upon joining battle with them.*[1]

---

[1] Καταστρατοπεδεύσας ἐπεῖχε τοῖς πολεμίοις, σπεύδων συμβαλεῖν εἰς μάχην. For the force of ἐπέχω in tactics, see the account of the battle of Cynossema in Thucydides (VIII. 105) with Arnold's note, Herodotus' description of the battle of Platæa (IX. 31, 59), and Arrian's of the battle

That these last words refer to the time when Hannibal and Scipio confronted each other on the banks of the Ticinus, cannot, I think, admit of question. But this march of Scipio, which terminated in his being opposed to Hannibal, is expressly synchronised by Polybius with a march of the Carthaginians, which terminated in Hannibal's arrival at the Insubrian country. From this fact, and also because it is certain that Hannibal and Scipio could never have confronted each other at any other part of Hannibal's route, I conclude that it is Hannibal's march to the Ticinus from the foot of the Alps which is described by the words of Polybius: κατῆρε τολμηρῶς εἰς τὰ περὶ τὸν Πάδον πεδία καὶ τὸ τῶν Ἰσόμβρων ἔθνος.

I add, for the purpose of comparison, the synchronistic movements of Hannibal and Scipio, as noticed by Polybius, and the same movements of the two generals as they are universally known:

I. Synchronistic movements described by Polybius:

---

of the Granicus (xiv. 4). Compare also *Odyss.* xxii. 75. Old editions of Polybius connect πολεμίοις, not with ἐπεῖχε, but with συμβαλεῖν εἰς μάχην, as if the punctuation were: καταστρατοπεδεύσας ἐπεῖχε, τοῖς πολεμίοις σπεύδων συμβαλεῖν εἰς μάχην. For the rendering which they give of the words is: castris positis substitit, cum hoste manus quam primum cupiens conserere. I believe this rendering is incorrect, but it would hardly affect my argument. For if Scipio, described in c. 49 as σπεύδων καταταχῆσαι τοὺς ὑπεναντίους πρὸς τὴν τῶν Ἄλπεων ὑπερβολήν, and again here as σπεύδων συμβαλεῖν εἰς μάχην—if he, bent upon these objects, encamped and *stopped*, we may safely infer that he was close upon Hannibal; that is to say, that he was upon the banks of the Ticinus, where the two armies met. Scipio never stopped till he arrived in those parts; and therefore Hannibal's arrival at the Insubrian country, which was contemporaneous with Scipio's stopping, would signify his arrival on the Ticinus after the capture of Turin.

I may notice, in reference to the site of the battle of the Ticinus, that Polybius (x. 3) fixes it near the Po (περὶ τὸν Πάδον καλούμενον ποταμόν).

HANNIBAL,	SCIPIO,
Having accomplished his march from New Carthage in five months,	Having left the management of the Spanish war to his brother, and sailed to Pisa,
And his passage of the Alps in fifteen days,	And having marched through Etruria, and procured an army,
Descended boldly into the plains of the Po,	Came to the plains of the Po,
And the country of the Insubres.	And encamped and opposed Hannibal.

II. Synchronistic movements, from the time of the action on the Rhone, universally known.

HANNIBAL,	SCIPIO,
Marched to the Island:	Returned to the Massilian coast:
Marched to the Alps:	Sailed to Pisa:
Crossed the Alps:	Crossed the Apennines:
Came to the plains of the Po:	Came to the plains of the Po:
Arrived on the Ticinus, and was opposed by Scipio.	Arrived on the Ticinus, and opposed Hannibal there.

The descent to the plains of the Po and the Insubrian country was, then, identical with the march from the foot of the Alps to the Ticinus, and brings us to the time when Hannibal and Scipio were opposed to one another, and on the point of joining battle on that river. This march to the Ticinus, after having been briefly noticed in c. 56, is described at length by Polybius in cc. 60—65. And this, as will be seen from the following comparison of the two authors, was the interpretation which Appian, whose narrative I shall give without omission, put upon Polybius:

POLYBIUS, c. 56.	APPIAN, vii. 5.

Τέλος δὲ, τὴν μὲν πᾶσαν πορείαν ἐκ Καινῆς πόλεως ἐν πέντε μησὶ ποιησάμενος, τὴν δὲ τῶν Ἄλπεων ὑπερβολὴν ἡμέραις πεντεκαίδεκα, κατῆρε τολμηρῶς εἰς τὰ περὶ τὸν

Πάδον πεδία, καὶ τὸ τῶν
Ἰσόμβρων ἔθνος.

Κατὰ δὲ τοὺς αὐτοὺς και
ροὺς, ὡς ἐπάνω προεῖπον,
Πόπλιος ἀπολελοιπὼς τὰς
δυνάμεις Γναίῳ τῷ ἀδελφῷ,
καὶ παρακεκληκὼς αὐτὸν ἔχ
εσθαι τῶν ἐν Ἰβηρίᾳ πραγ
μάτων, καὶ πολεμεῖν ἐῤῥω
μένως Ἀσδρούβᾳ,

κατέπλευσε μετ᾽ ὀλίγων αὐτὸς
εἰς Πίσας.

Ποιησάμενος δὲ τὴν πορείαν
διὰ Τυῤῥηνίας, καὶ παραλα
βὼν τὰ παρὰ τῶν ἐξεπελέ
κεων στρατόπεδα τὰ προκαθή
μενα καὶ προσπολεμοῦντα τοῖς
Βοίοις, ἧκε πρὸς τὰ περὶ τὸν
Πάδον πεδία,

καὶ καταστρατοπεδεύσας ἐπεῖ
χε τοῖς πολεμίοις, σπεύδων
συμβαλεῖν εἰς μάχην.

c. 65.

Ὁ μὲν οὖν Πόπλιος, προ
θέμενος τοὺς ἀκοντιστὰς, καὶ
τοὺς ἅμα τούτοις Γαλατικοὺς
ἱππεῖς, τοὺς δὲ λοιποὺς ἐν
μετώπῳ καταστήσας, προῄει
βάδην. Ὁ δ᾽ Ἀννίβας, κ.τ.λ.

τοιαύτην συνέβη γενέσθαι τὴν
πρώτην σύμπτωσιν, ὥστε τοὺς
ἀκοντιστὰς μὴ φθάσαι τὸ
πρῶτον ἐκβαλόντας βέλος,
κ. τ. λ. . . . .
Ὁμοῦ γὰρ ἦν ἱππομαχία
καὶ πεζομαχία, διὰ τὸ πλῆθος
τῶν παρακαταβαινόντων ἀν
δρῶν ἐν αὐτῇ τῇ μάχῃ. Τῶν
δὲ Νομάδων κυκλωσάντων, οἱ
μὲν πεζακοντισταὶ . . . . συνε

Ὁ δ᾽ ὕπατος ὁ Ῥωμαίων
Πούπλιος Κορνήλιος Σκιπίων,
Καρχηδονίοις ἐν Ἰβηρίᾳ πολε
μῶν, ἐπεὶ τῆς ἐσβολῆς Ἀννί
βου τῆς ἐς τὴν Ἰταλίαν ἐπύ
θετο, τὸν ἀδελφὸν καὶ ὅδε
Γναῖον Κορνήλιον Σκιπίωνα
ἐπὶ τοῖς ἐν Ἰβηρίᾳ πράγμασι
καταλιπών,
διέπλευσεν ἐς Τυῤῥηνίαν.

Ὅθεν ὁδεύων τε καὶ συμμά
χους ὅσους δύναιτο ἀγείρων,
ἔφθασεν ἐπὶ τὸν Πάδον Ἀννί
βαν. Καὶ Μάλλιον μὲν καὶ
Ἀτίλιον, οἳ τοῖς Βοίοις ἐπο
λέμουν, ἐς Ῥώμην ἔπεμψεν,
ὡς οὐ δέον αὐτοὺς στρατηγεῖν,
ὑπάτου παρόντος· αὐτὸς δὲ
τὸν στρατὸν παραλαβὼν
ἐς μάχην ἐξέτασσε πρὸς Ἀν
νίβαν.

Καὶ γενομένης ἀκροβολίας
τε

καὶ ἱππομαχίας

οἱ Ῥωμαῖοι κυκλωθέντες ὑπὸ
τῶν Λιβύων

πατήθησαν . . . . . οἱ δὲ . . . . . ἐπράπησαν, οἱ μὲν πολλοὶ σποράδες, τινὲς δὲ περὶ τὸν ἡγεμόνα συστραφέντες.	ἔφευγον ἐς τὸ στρατόπεδον.

c. 66.

Πόπλιος μὲν οὖν, ἀναζεύξας, προῆγε διὰ τῶν πεδίων ἐπὶ τὴν τοῦ Πάδου γέφυραν, σπεύδων φθᾶσαι διαβιβάσας τὰ στρατόπεδα.	Καὶ νυκτὸς ἐπιγενομένης
Ὁ δὲ Πόπλιος, περαιωθεὶς τὸν Πάδον, καὶ στρατοπεδεύσας περὶ πολιν Πλακεντίαν, κ. τ. λ.	ἐς Πλακεντίαν ἀνεχώρουν, κ. τ. λ.

I have now shewn, first by reference to the history of the movements of Hannibal and Scipio well known to every one, and then again by reference to Appian, that Hannibal's descent into the plains of the Po and the country of the Insubres refers to his march from the foot of the Alps to the Ticinus. I shall next shew the same by reference to Polybius' detailed narrative of that march from 'the very foot of the Alps' to the Ticinus, contained in cc. 60—65. The reader will, I believe, see without difficulty that the operations shortly mentioned in c. 56, and fully described in cc. 60—65, are identical.

c. 56.	c. 60.
Hannibal (having accomplished his march from New Carthage in five months, and his passage of the Alps in fifteen days) κατῆρε τολμηρῶς εἰς τὰ περὶ τὸν Πάδον πεδία,	Hannibal, having encamped ὑπ᾽ αὐτὴν τὴν παρώρειαν τῶν Ἄλπεων to give his army rest, proceeds, when they have recovered, to attack the chief town of the Taurini, οἳ τυγχάνουσι πρὸς τῇ παρωρείᾳ κατοικοῦντες. The town (Turin) is taken, and Hannibal's opponents slaughtered. The neighbouring tribes submit to Hannibal. Hannibal resolves to advance, and by some feat

καὶ τὸ τῶν Ἰσόμβρων ἔθνος.

of arms encourage his intended allies (Boii and Insubres) to join him, the greater part of them being then kept down by the presence of the Romans.

c. 61.

Hannibal hears that Scipio has passed the Po, and is near him. He at first disbelieves the report. Scipio is likewise astonished at the news of Hannibal's arrival.

cc. 62, 63.

Hannibal addresses and encourages his army.

c. 64.

Κατὰ δὲ τοὺς αὐτοὺς καιροὺς .... Πόπλιος .... ἧκε πρὸς τὰ περὶ τὸν Πάδον πεδία,

Πόπλιος δὲ περὶ τὰς αὐτὰς ἡμέρας, τὸν Πάδον ποταμὸν ἤδη πεπεραιω-μένος, τὸν δὲ Τίκινον κρί-νων εἰς τοὔμπροσθεν διαβαί-νειν, τοῖς μὲν ἐπιτηδείοις γε-φυροποιεῖν παρήγγειλε, τὰς δὲ λοιπὰς δυνάμεις συναγαγὼν παρεκάλει. Scipio was here in the Ἰσόμβρων ἔθνος. After giving an account of Scipio's speech, Polybius thus resumes his narrative:—

c. 65.

καὶ καταστρατοπεδεύσας

Τῇ δὲ κατὰ πόδας ἡμέρᾳ προῆγον ἀμφότεροι παρὰ τὸν ποταμόν, ἐκ τοῦ πρὸς τὰς Ἄλ-πεις μέρους, ἔχοντες εὐώνυμον μὲν οἱ Ῥωμαῖοι, δεξιὸν δὲ τὸν ῥοῦν οἱ Καρχηδόνιοι. Γνόντες δὲ τῇ δευτέρᾳ διὰ τῶν προνο-μευόντων ὅτι σύνεγγύς εἰσιν ἀλλήλων, τότε μὲν αὐτοῦ καταστρατοπεδεύσαντες ἔμειναν. Τῇ δ' ἐπαύριον πᾶ-σαν τὴν ἵππον ἀναλαβόντες ἀμφότεροι, Πόπλιος δὲ καὶ

τῶν πεζῶν τοὺς ἀκοντιστάς,
προῆγον διὰ τοῦ πεδίου, σπεύ-
δοντες κατοπτεῦσαι τὰς
ἀλλήλων δυνάμεις. "Αμα
δὲ τῷ πλησιάζειν αὐτοῖς, καὶ
συνιδεῖν τὸν κονιορτὸν ἐξαιρό-
μενον, εὐθέως συνετάττον-
ἐπεῖχε τοῖς πολεμίοις,   το πρὸς μάχην. Ὁ μὲν
οὖν Πόπλιος, προθέμενος τοὺς
ἀκοντιστάς, καὶ τοὺς ἅμα τούτοις Γαλατικοὺς ἱππεῖς, τοὺς
δὲ λοιποὺς ἐν μετώπῳ καταστήσας, προῄει βάδην. Ὁ δ᾽
Ἀννίβας, τὴν μὲν κεχαλινω-
μένην ἵππον καὶ πᾶν τὸ στά-
σιμον αὐτῆς κατὰ πρόσωπον
τάξας, ἀπήντα τοῖς πολεμίοις,
τοὺς δὲ Νομαδικοὺς ἱππεῖς
ἀφ᾽ ἑκατέρου τοῦ κέρατος ἡτοι-
μάκει πρὸς κύκλωσιν. Ἀμ-
σπεύδων συμβαλεῖν εἰς μά-   φοτέρων δὲ καὶ τῶν ἡμε-
χην.   μόνων καὶ τῶν ἱππέων
φιλοτίμως διακειμένων
πρὸς τὸν κίνδυνον, τοιαύ-
την συνέβη γενέσθαι τὴν πρώτην σύμπτωσιν, κ. τ. λ.

It will be perceived that the events narrated in
cc. 60—65 might be briefly described by the expressions of c. 56. For, in the march from the foot of the
Alps to the Ticinus, as narrated in cc. 60—65, Hannibal certainly κατῆρε——τολμηρῶς (cf. especially ἔκρινε
.....πράττειν τι, end of c. 60)——εἰς τὰ περὶ τὸν
Πάδον πεδία——καὶ τὸ τῶν Ἰσόμβρων ἔθνος; while Scipio
as certainly, as is likewise mentioned in c. 56, ἧκε πρὸς
τὰ περὶ τὸν Πάδον πεδία——καὶ καταστρατοπεδεύσας——
ἐπεῖχε τοῖς πολεμίοις——σπεύδων συμβαλεῖν εἰς μάχην.
It is incredible that Hannibal could have made two
marches to the Insubrian country, both beginning at
the same point, the edge of the plains, both of a similar
character, and both terminating by his being met by

Scipio. Above all, it is incredible how, according to the Bernardine theory, this first descent to the In- subrian country could have begun and terminated near Ivrea, the point which they would have to fix on for the encampment of Hannibal at the beginning of c. 60. For let us for one moment take this hypothesis for granted, and admit that what is men- tioned in c. 56 precedes, instead of being identical with, what is related in cc. 60—65.

As Scipio has encamped and opposed Hannibal, with the view of giving battle as soon as possible, in c. 56, and as Hannibal is, at the beginning of c. 60, found encamped at the very foot of the Alps, *i. e.* according to the Bernardine hypothesis, somewhere near Ivrea, we should have to suppose that the two generals were encamped against one another near that town. Now let us see what Scipio, being eager for battle, proceeds to do. He first allows Hannibal's army, encamped ὑπ' αὐτὴν τὴν παρώρειαν τῶν Ἄλπεων, to recover from its debilitated condition. He next allows Hannibal to send messengers with overtures of amity and alliance to the Taurini, 'who happen,' (or, as we must read on the Bernardine theory, 'who do *not* happen') 'to dwell πρὸς τῇ παρωρείᾳ.' When these overtures are rejected, Scipio must also allow the Carthaginian army to march by or through his camp, to besiege and take Turin, and to receive the submission of the Taurini and the neighbouring tribes. We must also be prepared to find that, after all this, Hannibal and Scipio were ignorant of each other's presence in Italy ; and that Scipio, after having encamped against Hannibal near Ivrea, should next be found, some weeks after, crossing the Po near Placentia into the Milanese, and meeting Hannibal,

on the advance of the Carthaginians from Turin, upon
the Ticinus. These singular proceedings result from
the Bernardine theory, and from the manner in which
its advocates interpret c. 56, when that theory and
interpretation are carried out to their legitimate conclusion.

The descent to the plains of the Po and the country
of the Insubres, as mentioned in c. 56, being thus
identical with the march from the foot of the Alps to
the Ticinus, described in cc. 60—65, the words,
κατῆρε τολμηρῶς εἰς τὰ περὶ τόν Πάδον πεδία καὶ τὸ τῶν
Ἰσόμβρων ἔθνος, must therefore be regarded, as I have
mentioned elsewhere,[1] as " a succinct account or summary, merely stating the direction and end of a march,
the details of which are afterwards to be given." If
we interpret it otherwise, and thus make two marches
instead of one, we reduce the narrative of Polybius,
as I have just shewn, to a tissue of absurdities. The
two marches must be the same; and the first or
succinct account is given by the historian in order
that the object and character of the operations afterwards narrated at length may be clearly understood.

Several passages may be adduced where the destination of a march or journey is named in a similar
manner by way of anticipation. The following are in
Polybius. In the first the mode of expression is very
like that adopted in the notice of the march to the
Insubrian country.

1. Διόπερ Ἀννίβας, ὁρῶν τὸν Φάβιον φυγομαχοῦντα
μὲν προδήλως, τοῖς δ' ὅλοις οὐκ ἐκχωροῦντα τῶν ὑπαίθρων,
ὥρμησε τολμηρῶς εἰς τὰ περὶ Καπύην πεδία, καὶ
τούτων εἰς τὸν προσαγορευόμενον Φάλερνον τόπον.
(III. 90. Hannibal reaches his destination in III. 92).

---

[1] *Treatise on Hannibal's Passage of the Alps*, p. 61.

2. Κατὰ δὲ τοὺς καιροὺς τούτους ἐκ Σαρδόνος μετὰ τῶν στρατοπέδων Γάϊος Ἀτίλιος ὕπατος εἰς Πίσας καταπεπλευκὼς, προῆγε μετὰ τῆς δυνάμεως εἰς Ῥώμην, ἐναντίαν ποιούμενος τοῖς πολεμίοις τὴν πορείαν (II. 27. Atilius (II. 28) was killed in battle at Telamon, rather more than half-way between Pisa and Rome).

3. Τὴν δὲ λοιπὴν στρατιὰν ἀναλαβὼν εὔζωνον, πεζοὺς μὲν πεντακισμυρίους, ἱππεῖς δὲ πρὸς ἐννακισχιλίους, ἦγε διὰ τῶν Πυρηναίων λεγομένων ὀρῶν, ἐπὶ τὴν τοῦ Ῥοδανοῦ καλουμένου ποταμοῦ διάβασιν. (III. 35. Hannibal reaches the Pyrenees in III. 40, and the Rhone in III. 41).

To these parallel passages from Polybius, two may be added from Herodotus:

1. Ὁ πεζὸς ἅπας συλλελεγμένος, ἅμα Ξέρξῃ ἐπορεύετο ἐς Σάρδις, εκ Κριτάλλων ὁρμηθεὶς τῶν ἐν Καππαδοκίῃ. (VII. 26. Xerxes reaches Sardis in VII. 31.)

2. Ὁ στρατὸς ἐκ τῶν Σαρδίων ὡρμᾶτο ἐλῶν ἐς Ἄβυδον (VII. 37. Abydus is reached in VII. 44).

I subjoin two other familiar instances:

1. Καὶ ἐξῆλθεν Ἰακὼβ ἀπὸ τοῦ φρέατος τοῦ ὅρκου· καὶ ἐπορεύθη εἰς Χαρράν (Gen. xxviii. 10. Haran is reached in c. xxix).

2. Ἀφῆκε τὴν Ἰουδαίαν, καὶ ἀπῆλθε πάλιν εἰς τὴν Γαλιλαίαν (John iv. 3. Galilee is reached in iv. 45. Samaria intervened between Judæa and Galilee, as the country of the Taurini (and that of the Libui) lay between the Alps and the Insubrian territory).

The account given by Polybius, in c. 56, of the operations of Hannibal and Scipio, which terminate with the meeting of the two generals in 'the country of the Insubres', has now been compared with the known course of the movements of the Romans and Carthaginians, with the narrative of Appian, and with the context in Polybius himself. Let us finally, in order to exhaust the evidence, institute a comparison between Polybius and Livy, and thus derive a fourth argument for assuming that Hannibal's arrival at the Insubrian country was posterior to the siege of Turin and the transactions with the Taurini.

POLYBIUS.

While Hannibal, after having crossed the Alps, descended boldly into the plains of the Po and the Insubrian country, Scipio, having sailed to Pisa, and taken the command of the army of the prætors, came to the plains of the Po and opposed Hannibal, to whom he was eager to give battle (c. 56).

After having encamped, on his entry into Italy, at the very foot of the Alps, Hannibal made to the Taurini, who dwelt there, offers of amity and alliance. On receiving a refusal, having laid siege to their chief city, he took it in three days; and, having slaughtered his opponents, so terrified the neighbouring barbarians that they came at once and made submission: while the rest of the Gauls inhabiting the plains were desirous of joining Hannibal, as they had originally intended; but as the Romans had passed through their country, and cut most of them off (from Hannibal), they remained quiet, and some were even obliged to fight on the Roman side (c. 60).

LIVY, XXI. 39.

Ea P. Cornelio consuli causa fuit, cum Pisas navibus venisset, exercitu a Manlio Atilioque accepto tirone et in novis ignominiis trepido, ad Padum festinandi ut cum hoste nondum refecto manus sereret. Sed cum Placentiam consul venit [and therefore before Scipio opposed Hannibal in the Insubrian country], jam ex stativis *moverat* Hannibal, Taurinorumque unam urbem, caput gentis ejus, quia volentes in amicitiam non veniebant, vi *expugnarat;* junxissetque sibi, non metu solo sed etiam voluntate, Gallos accolas Padi, ni eos circumspectantes defectionis tempus subito adventus consulis oppressisset.

These Gauls, who wished to join Hannibal, but were mostly cut off by the Romans, were the Insubres and Boii. Of these the Insubres were nearest to Hannibal, and their country is therefore mentioned in c. 56, as the point to which Hannibal marched from the foot of the Alps. It is hardly possible, on this ground alone, that Hannibal, as the Bernardine theory would assume, joined the Insubres before the siege of Turin; and had he joined them then, a considerable time before the action on the Ticinus, he ought clearly not to have marched from the Milanese against Turin, and so have allowed the Romans to deprive him of his allies. With their assistance, or even without, he might have overwhelmed or expelled the forces of the prætors before Scipio came up from Etruria.

I hope I have now satisfactorily shewn that the words of Polybius, κατῆρε τολμηρῶς κ. τ. λ., refer to Hannibal's march to the Ticinus, and are therefore "a succinct account or summary, merely stating the direction and end of a march, the details of which are afterwards to be given." And I believe that a similar account may be rendered of all the other passages in the narrative of Polybius, which in my first work on this subject I have called "summaries." I here subjoin them in the Greek, with the explanation I give of them; and I think it will be seen that they present to us briefly the whole march of Hannibal, from the time that he crossed the Rhone to the time of his arrival on the Ticinus.

49. v.—'Αννίβας δὲ ποιησάμενος ἑξῆς ἐπὶ τέτταρας ἡμέρας τὴν πορείαν ἀπὸ τῆς διαβάσεως, ἧκε πρὸς τὴν καλουμένην Νῆσον, χώραν πολύοχλον καὶ σιτοφόρον, ἔχουσαν δὲ τὴν προσηγορίαν ἀπ' αὐτοῦ τοῦ συμπτώματος.

March from the passage of the Rhone to the Island (at the confluence of the Rhone and Isère), four days.

50. I.—'Αννίβας δ' ἐν ἡμέ-

March from the confluence

ραις δέκα πορευθεὶς παρὰ τὸν
ποταμὸν εἰς ὀκτακοσίους σταδίους, ἤρξατο τῆς πρὸς τὰς
Ἄλπεις ἀναβολῆς, καὶ συνέβη μεγίστοις αὐτὸν περι-
πεσεῖν κινδύνοις.

52. II.—Ταῖς δ' ἑξῆς, μέχρι
μέν τινος ἀσφαλῶς διῆγε τὴν
στρατιάν· ἤδη δὲ τεταρταῖος
ὤν, αὖθις εἰς κινδύνους
παρεγένετο μεγάλους.

53. VI.—Τῇ δ' ἐπαύριον,
τῶν πολεμίων χωρισθέντων,
συνάψας τοῖς ἱππεῦσι καὶ
τοῖς ὑποζυγίοις, προῆγε
πρὸς τὰς ὑπερβολὰς τὰς
ἀνωτάτω τῶν Ἄλπεων,
ὁλοσχερεῖ μὲν οὐδενὶ περιπίπ-
των ἔτι συστήματι τῶν βαρ-
βάρων, κατὰ μέρη δὲ καὶ κατὰ
τόπους παρενοχλούμενος ὑπ'
αὐτῶν.

53. IX.—Ἐνναταῖος δὲ δια-
νύσας εἰς τὰς ὑπερβολὰς, αὐτοῦ κατεστρατοπέδευσε
καὶ δύο ἡμέρας προσέ-
μεινε· βουλόμενος ἅμα μὲν
ἀναπαῦσαι τοὺς διασωζομέ-
νους, ἅμα δὲ προσδέξασθαι
τοὺς ὑπολειπομένους.

54. IV.—Τῇ δ' ἐπαύριον
ἀναζεύξας, ἐνήρχετο τῆς
καταβάσεως, ἐν ᾗ πολε-
μίοις μὲν οὐκ ἔτι περιέτυχε,
πλὴν τῶν λάθρα κακοποιούν-
των ὑπὸ δὲ τῶν τόπων καὶ τῆς
χιόνος, οὐ πολλῷ λείποντας
ἀπέβαλε τῶν κατὰ τὴν ἀνά-
βασιν φθαρέντων.

56. III.—Τέλος δὲ, τὴν μὲν
πᾶσαν πορείαν ἐκ Καινῆς πόλεως ἐν πέντε μησὶ ποιησάμενος, τὴν δὲ τῶν Ἄλπεων ὑπερβολὴν ἡμέραις πεντεκαίδεκα,
κατῆρε τολμηρῶς εἰς τὰ
περὶ τὸν Πάδον πεδία, καὶ
τὸ τῶν Ἰσόμβρων ἔθνος.

of the Rhone and Isère to the
battle (near the Town of the
Allobroges) at the commencement of the Alps, ten days.

March from the Town of
the Allobroges to the battle
at the Leucopetron, four days
from the Town (the first four
days of the Alpine march).

March from the Leucope-
tron to the summit of the
Alps, beginning on the day
after the fourth day from the
Town, and terminating (see
next passage) on the ninth
day from the same place.

Halt on the summit of the
Alps, ninth and tenth days
from the Town.

March from the summit of
the Alps to their foot, beginning on the day after the
tenth day from the Town, and
terminating (see next passage)
on the fifteenth day from the
same place.

March from the foot of the
Alps to the Insubrian country,
i. e. to the Ticinus.

I think this comparison alone may be sufficient to bear out what I said in my first work (p. 6) upon this subject :

"There is however, one peculiarity in Polybius' style of narration, especially in this part of his history, upon which it will previously be necessary to make some observations. The peculiarity alluded to is this : that the historian, before entering into the details of a particular march, event, or military transaction, gives, in a few lines, what may be regarded as a short statement or summary of the occurrences which took place at that particular period. Having done this, he proceeds to make such observations, and give such explanations, as appear necessary, or to narrate at length the various circumstances that attended the facts in question, whenever they were of such importance as to deserve minute consideration. The short summary serves frequently, in point of fact, as an argument to the succeeding and more detailed account."

4. The fourth point I undertook to shew was this:

The plains of the Taurini are twice placed by Polybius at the foot of Hannibal's Alps; and the same opinion was universally held by the ancients : so that Hannibal must of necessity have crossed the Cottian Alps.

This is very shortly proved, as far as Polybius' history is concerned (III. 60). On Hannibal's entry into Italy, he encamped at the very foot of the Alps, in order that his army might rest, and recover from their hardships in the mountains. Μετὰ τὴν εἰσβολὴν, κατα-στρατοπεδεύσας ὑπ' αὐτὴν τὴν παρώρειαν τῶν Ἀλ-πεων, τὰς μὲν ἀρχὰς ἀνελάμβανε τὰς δυνάμεις. As soon as his army had recovered, προσανειληφυίας ἤδη τῆς δυνάμεως, Hannibal made offers of amity and alliance to the Taurini, "who are found dwelling at the mountain-foot," οἳ τυγχάνουσι πρὸς τῇ παρωρείᾳ κατοικοῦντες. As the παρώρεια of this second passage is clearly identical with the παρώρεια of the first, and as the first παρώρεια is as clearly that of the Alps which Hannibal crossed, it follows that the Taurini dwelt at the foot of the Alps of Hannibal.

I do not think that the manner in which Messrs. Wickham and Cramer meet this passage, will diminish in any way the obvious force of it. They deal with it, as I find, three times, which I shall now proceed to notice.

The first time is at p. 107, where they derive from it the following statement:

"Finding that the Taurini were at war with his allies, the Insubres, he (Hannibal) made overtures of reconciliation to them."

But Polybius wrote:

"After this, his army having now recovered its condition (in the encampment ὑπ' αὐτὴν τὴν παρώρειαν τῶν Ἄλπεων, *i.e.* at the foot of the Alps which Hannibal crossed), as the Taurini, who happen to dwell πρὸς τῇ παρωρείᾳ (*i.e.* at that mountain-foot), were at feud (or war) with the Insubres and (thus) distrusted the Carthaginians, he made overtures of amity and alliance (φιλία καὶ συμμαχία) to them."

Now, in the first place, amity and alliance with the Carthaginians ought not to have been changed into reconciliation with the Insubres. Yet this is of comparatively little importance. But Messrs. W. and C. should not have omitted the significant description which Polybius gives of the position of the Taurini, "at the mountain-foot"; not merely because M. Letronne, whom they profess to answer later, had appealed to it, but also because their object here was (p. 108) "to explain the error into which those writers have fallen, who have supposed Hannibal to have arrived first among the Taurini." For the origin of this so-called error is not explained by omitting the words on which it is founded.

On the second occasion when this passage is dealt with, it is in order to confute Livy, whom they make to say, as he does in substance : "Now it is agreed on all hands that he (Hannibal) arrived among the Taurini after crossing the Alps."

To this Messrs. W. and C. reply (p. 147):

" Certainly not, according to Polybius, who *states positively*, that after having refreshed his troops by a few days' halt, he entered boldly into the country of the Insubres."

This singular statement is obtained by combining together fragments of the two following well-known sentences in Polybius, the first sentence being in c. 60, and the second in c. 56 :

Μετὰ δὲ ταῦτα, προσανειληφυίας ἤδη τῆς δυνάμεως, τῶν Ταυρινῶν, οἱ τυγχάνουσι πρὸς τῇ παρωρείᾳ
κατοικοῦντες, στασιαζόντων μὲν πρὸς τοὺς Ἰσομβρας, ἀπι-
στοῦντων δὲ τοῖς Καρχηδονίοις, τὸ μὲν πρῶτον αὐτοὺς εἰς
φιλίαν προυκαλεῖτο καὶ συμμαχίαν· οὐχ ὑπακουόντων δὲ,
περιστρατοπεδεύσας τὴν βαρυτάτην πόλιν, ἐν τρισὶν ἡμέραις
ἐξεπολιόρκησε[1] (c. 60).

Τέλος δὲ, τὴν μὲν πᾶσαν πορείαν ἐκ Καινῆς πόλεως ἐν
πέντε μησὶ ποιησάμενος, τὴν δὲ τῶν Ἄλπεων ὑπερβολὴν
ἡμέραις πεντεκαίδεκα, κατῆρε τολμηρῶς εἰς τὰ περὶ τὸν
Πάδον πεδία, καὶ τὸ τῶν Ἰσόμβρων ἔθνος (c. 56).

By combining the parts which I have particularly indicated of these two sentences, and by changing in the latter the word κατῆρε for εἰσῆλθε, Messrs. W. and C. are enabled to make Polybius *state positively*, in opposition to Livy, that Hannibal, "having refreshed his troops by a few days' halt, entered boldly into the

---

[1] Observe here that Turin was probably near the encampment of Hannibal, as no march upon the capital of the Taurini is noticed.

country of the Insubres." Yet it must be apparent
to every one who reads the 60th chapter of Polybius,
that when Hannibal had refreshed his troops by a few
days' halt, he entered boldly into the country of the
Taurini. The agreement between Polybius and Livy
is perfect. Polybius places the Taurini at the foot of
the Alps which Hannibal crossed; and Livy says that
Hannibal came down into Italy among the Taurini,
who were the nearest people to Gaul, and also the
first people that Hannibal came to in Italy ("Taurinis,
proximæ genti, adversus Insubres motum bellum erat"
XXI. 39). Cf. Liv. XXVII. 18: "Proximus Cartha-
giniensium exercitus Hasdrubalis prope urbem Bæcu-
lam erat."

The third occasion on which Messrs W. and C.
have to deal with the passage relating to the Taurini,
is in their answer to M. Letronne, who considered
that Hannibal crossed the Mont Genèvre (p. 153).
Here they first accuse him of " preferring to take his
author (Polybius) at secondhand in Strabo, to reading
him in his own words;" and then, on the same page,
annul the strength of this charge by the words: " He
positively quotes Polybius as his authority for saying,
that the Taurini were the first people whom Hannibal
met with on his descent from the Alps; and this
authority he finds in the sixtieth chapter." M.
Letronne is no doubt guilty of this last accusation, for
he expressly refers to the eighth section of the sixtieth
chapter, where the position of the Taurini is described,
in support of his argument. From the words describing this position, which he interprets very accurately,
he concludes, "que les Taurini furent les premiers
peuples qu' Annibal rencontra à la descente des Alpes"
(τῶν Ταυρινῶν, οἳ τυγχάνουσι πρὸς τῇ παρωρείᾳ κατοικοῦν-

τες); to which the only answer that Messrs. W. and
C. think it advisable to give him is: "If by this
violence committed on the text of one of his authors,
M. L(etronne) was in any degree assisted in his
hypothesis, some excuse might be found for him."

Considering the manner in which Messrs. W. and
C. have treated the passage which M. Letronne ap-
peals to, on the second occasion when they deal with
it, it must be confessed that "committing violence on
the text of an author" was a very unfortunate phrase
for them to use. And, when we remember how they
have dealt with it the first time, the following sentence (p. 153) is no less unhappy: "Although it is far
from our intention to charge M. L(etronne) with bad
faith, it certainly behoved him to be extremely careful
not to lay himself open to the charge of a wilful omission
of the text of his author, at the very moment when he
was accusing M. De Luc of the same fault."   M. De
Luc had cited the words of Polybius in Strabo, τὴν
(ὑπέρβασιν) διὰ Ταυρινῶν, ἣν Ἀννίβας διῆλθεν, with the
omission of what relates to Hannibal; and M. Letronne
had not noticed the words, κατῆρε τολμηρῶς κ. τ. λ.,
which have, however, nothing to do with the place
where Hannibal crossed the Alps, though it might
have been better for M. Letronne to have intimated as
much.

It is in the above manner that Messrs. W. and C.
have dealt with the passage in question.   One argument which they bring forward (p. 123) in opposition
to the opinion, that the Taurini dwelt at the foot of
Hannibal's Alps, may be deserving of a passing notice:

"Would Hannibal, on entering a territory whose inclina-
tions to him were at least doubtful, have dispersed his army,
and left himself entirely without defence, *in the manner
described by Polybius?*

This is pure imagination. For Polybius affirms that Hannibal refreshed his army, κατaστρατοπεδεύσας ὑπ' αὐτὴν τὴν παρωρείαν τῶν Ἄλπεων (c. 60). Now an army encamped, and resting on the Alps, is neither dispersed, nor left entirely without defence. Indeed, Hannibal's not advancing from this position, though with predatory mountaineers behind him, till his army had recovered, rather intimates that he was on the edge of a doubtful or hostile, and not a friendly and allied country.

The second occasion on which Polybius places the Taurini at the foot of the Alps of Hannibal, is noticed by Strabo (p. 209). I will here quote what Messrs. Wickham and Cramer say upon the subject (p. 16):

" Strabo informs us that Polybius, who is the earliest authority on the subject, mentions only four passages over the Alps."

" 'The first, through the Ligurians, close to the Tyrrhenian Sea; the second, through the country of the Taurini, *which Hannibal traversed;* the third, through that of the Salassi; the fourth, over the Rhætian Alps—all precipitous.' With regard to this passage of Strabo, it is necessary to observe, that it contains a positive assertion, that Hannibal passed by the road leading through the country of the Taurini; and if this assertion was made by Polybius, *it ought certainly to be considered as decisive of the question, which it is the object of this dissertation to determine.* But the best proof that can be offered against this conclusion, and in favour of the opinion that the words, ἦν 'Αννίβας διῆλθεν, are Strabo's own, is furnished by Polybius himself, who *positively asserts* (l. 3, c. 56) that Hannibal descended among the Insubrians, before he invaded the territory of the Taurini; consequently, he could not have stated that he passed the Alps of the latter, without contradicting himself."

As I have already shewn that this last ' positive assertion' of Polybius is not in that author, but is merely a false inference, inconsistent with the context, of Messrs. W. and C. themselves, the citation from Polybius in Strabo " ought certainly to be considered as decisive of the question." But Messrs. W. and C. have another argument against the genuineness of the words, ἣν Ἀννίβας διῆλθεν. "If Polybius," they say (p. 17), "had expressly named the passage by which he affirmed that Hannibal had crossed the Alps, it would not have been a subject of doubt and controversy, as Livy asserts it to have been, when he was writing his history." But Polybius does not expressly name the pass which Hannibal crossed, in spite of Strabo's word, ὀνομάζει. A pass is expressly named when it is called, for instance, the Cenis or the Simplon; but not when the route is merely described as leading through Savoy or the Vallais. What Polybius affirmed of Hannibal's pass was, that it traversed the country of the Taurini; and this is so far from being disputed by Livy, that he represents it as acknowledged by all (inter omnes constat), which was the last thing I undertook to prove.

For Livy (xxi. 38) relates that L. Cincius Alimentus, who was a prisoner of Hannibal's, declared in his history that he had heard *from Hannibal himself* that the Carthaginian losses amounted to 36,000 men, between the time of Hannibal's crossing the Rhone, and his descent into Italy by the country of the Taurini, who were the nearest people to Gaul (Taurinis, quæ Gallis proxima gens erat, in Italiam degressum). And then Livy continues: " *Id (Taurinis Hannibalem in Italiam degressum esse) cum inter omnes constet,* eo magis miror ambigi quanam Alpes transierit, et vulgo credere Penino (atque inde nomen ei jugo Alpium inditum) transgressum, Cœlium per Cremonis jugum dicere transisse ; *qui ambo saltus eum non in Taurinos, sed per Salassos montanos ad Libuos Gallos deduxissent.*" It must be evident to all, that Livy, so far from contradicting the words ascribed by Strabo to Polybius (εἶτα τὴν (ὑπέρβασιν) διὰ Ταυρινῶν, ἣν ᾿Αννίβας διῆλθεν), exactly confirms them, and asserts that the fact of Hannibal's passage through the country of the Taurini was universally acknowledged. Nor are we necessarily to infer, that even Cœlius and the ancient Bernardine advocates denied that the Taurini lay at the foot of Hannibal's Alps. It may be said, perhaps, that it would be a strange geographical error for them to make. True: but their error with respect to the Taurini would be no worse than what the modern Bernardine advocates make with respect to the Insubres. Indeed, it would be hardly so bad : for Ivrea, where the Bernardine route enters the Italian plain, is rather nearer to Turin, the Taurine capital, than it is to Novara, the frontier town of the Insubres, which was 49 M. P. from Ivrea. Yet we cannot assume that Messrs. Wickham and Cramer, M. De Luc, and Mr. Law, do not hold that the Insubres lay at the foot of Hannibal's Alps, although they are inconsistent enough to argue that Hannibal crossed the Little St. Bernard, which he could not have done in such a case.

CHAPTER II.

FURTHER OBJECTIONS AGAINST THE OPINION THAT HANNIBAL CROSSED
THE LITTLE ST. BERNARD.

I NOW come to what, if Polybius may be believed,
forms a second insuperable objection against the Little
St. Bernard. It depends on the time occupied in the
descent to the plains. Here Polybius gives us two
accounts; one of detail, one of brief recapitulation.
He first states that Hannibal fell into great danger
on the 4th day of his Alpine march, and that he
reached the crest of the Alps on the 9th day. There
he remained two days, the 9th and 10th days, the day
of arrival being included, as is allowed by Messrs. W.
and C. (p. 114). The same principle of inclusion is
afterwards observed. Hannibal thus begins to descend
on the 11th day, and is stopped by the loss of his
path before he has passed beyond the regions of snow.
This happened on the same 11th day, as is admitted
(p. 111). After an ineffectual attempt to turn the
broken path, Hannibal sets to work to repair it; makes
it practicable in one day for the cavalry; and, after
having suffered the hardships of this enforced halt
during three days, succeeds in making the elephants
pass by the repaired road. These three days of suffering were the 11th, 12th, and 13th days. On the
third day from that on which the elephants passed,

i. e. from the 13th day, Hannibal reaches the plains.
He would therefore reach them on the 15th day.
This is the detailed account of Polybius. In his
recapitulation he says that Hannibal accomplished
the passage of the Alps in fifteen days. Both accounts given by Polybius are therefore strictly in accordance with each other. Now it seems plain that if
the Carthaginians were exposed to suffering by their
compulsory stoppage at or close to La Thuile, according to Messrs. W. and C., during the three days which
were the 11th, 12th and 13th days, they could not
have left La Thuile before the evening of the 13th
day, or have commenced their march from Pré St.
Didier, six miles below, before the 14th morning.
Here the whole army would be again reunited, and
would consequently only have two clear days in which
to perform the journey between Pré St. Didier and
the commencement of the plains near Ivrea, a distance
of about 70 Roman miles.[1] That they could have
performed such a distance in two days is impossible.

Let us now see how this difficulty is attempted to
be overcome. First then, the commencement of the
plains is moved back twelve Roman miles from Ivrea
to St. Martin, at the head of the lowest reach of the
valley of Aosta. This seems inadmissible. The
commencement of the plains of the Po can hardly be
fixed at the upper extremity of such a reach, merely
because the reach happens to be nearly level. Nor
is the following argument (p. 119) more tenable:
'Another reason which will prevent our pushing it
(the commencement of the plains) further (than St.

---

[1] By the Roman Itineraries the distance between Arebrigium and
Eporedia was 71 M.P. By the Sardinian Itinerary the distance from Pré
St. Didier to Ivrea = 68½ M.P.

Martin), is the distance to be performed by the army, in their descent of three days, after the passage of the rocks near La Tuille.' This is an obvious *petitio principii*. The theory of the Little St. Bernard cannot be sustained, it is thought, unless the commencement of the plains be fixed at St. Martin. Therefore it is to be fixed at St. Martin.

But that theory cannot stand, even if the commencement of the plains be so fixed: and therefore let such an arrangement be admitted for the sake of argument. The authors place St. Martin 12 M. P. above Ivrea, and therefore, according to the Roman Itineraries, 59 M. P. from Arebrigium, which they identify with Pré St. Didier. The Sardinian Itinerary gives the distance between Ivrea and Pré St. Didier at 68½ M. P., which would give 56½ M. P. between St. Martin and Pré St. Didier. The ancient distance of 59 M. P. would therefore probably be correct. Messrs. W. and C. reduce it to about 55 M. P., on the ground that they could not otherwise have been driven as far as they were in the time their ride occupied. But let the distance be 55 M. P. The argument then proceeds thus (p. 119):

" From Pré St. Didier to St. Martin, we have about fifty-five Roman miles, which make about eighteen miles a-day."

The authors thus assume that Polybius would allow them three full days from Pré St. Didier to the commencement of the plains: it is thus they interpret, τριταῖος ἀπὸ τῶν προειρημένων κρημνῶν διανύσας ἥψατο τῶν ἐπιπέδων. Hannibal reaches the plains on the third day after leaving La Thuile, and therefore has three clear days from Pré St. Didier, 6 M. P. below La Thuile. But this would require τεταρταῖος, not

D

τριταῖος. Hannibal starts from La Thuile on the afternoon of the 13th day, and reaches the plains on the
15th. He has therefore only two days between Pré
St. Didier and St. Martin, and the marches would be
of about 28 or 30 miles, according as we take the
distances of Messrs. W. and C. or of the Roman
Itineraries. But let us see how the case stands on
the authors' own shewing:

"From Pré St. Didier to St. Martin, we have about fifty-
five Roman miles, which make about eighteen miles a-day,
*too long a march, certainly, for troops in the fatigued and
shattered condition of the Carthaginian army.*"

The theory of the Little St. Bernard, then, still
fails, marches of eighteen miles a-day being about
one-third too much. Messrs W. and C. therefore
make another supposition:

"In point of fact, however, the cavalry and infantry had
six days instead of three, to perform this march in, since they
had three clear days, during the time the road was preparing
for the elephants," who "might have arrived at St. Martin
a day or two later, as they were much exhausted."

The cavalry and infantry would have passed La
Thuile on the 12th day, and would therefore, on this
supposition, reach St. Martin on the 18th: *i. e.* a part
only of the Carthaginian army succeeds in reaching
the plains on the 18th day. But how can this be
true, or how could the cavalry and infantry reach the
plains on the sixth day from Pré St. Didier, or the
seventh from La Thuile, when the passage of the
Alps was effected in fifteen days, and the cavalry and
infantry did not leave La Thuile till the 12th day?
The first remedy which Messrs W. and C. propose in
this case is a violent one, nothing less than an altera-
tion in the text of Polybius. They say (p. 115):

"I (we) think that there can be very little doubt that we must read *eighteen* days instead of *fifteen*"—"for (p. 116) there can be no doubt, upon his (Polybius') own shewing, that eighteen days must have elapsed before this event took place."

I have already proved that this last statement is not correct, as the number of days in Polybius' detailed account need not amount to more than fifteen. I have also explained how Polybius' "three days of hardship" extended from the middle of the 11th to the middle of the 13th day, and that Hannibal was consequently detained near the broken path no more than two full days. Messrs. W. and C. extend the time of detention to four full days, apparently following Livy's error, "quatriduum circa rupem consumptum." Yet Livy might have shewn them that the text of Polybius was correct as to the πεντεκαίδεκα; for Livy says:

'*Quinto mense* a Carthagine nova, ut *quidam auctores* sunt, *quinto decimo die* Alpibus superatis.'

I believe there can be no doubt that this is taken from Polybius'—

Τὴν μὲν πᾶσαν πορείαν ἐκ Καινῆς πόλεως ἐν πέντε μησὶ ποιησάμενος, τὴν δὲ τῶν Ἄλπεων ὑπερβολὴν ἡμέραις πεντεκαίδεκα.

The supposition of an error in the text of Polybius is therefore inadmissible. But the argument of the authors would also fail on other grounds, for they assume that the cavalry and infantry, when they had passed La Thuile on the 12th day, did not wait a little below for Hannibal and the rest of the army, but marched on in a separate body to the plains. Yet Polybius tells us that Hannibal united together *his whole army* before he descended to the plains:

'Αννίβας δὲ, συναθροίσας ὁμοῦ πᾶσαν τὴν δύναμιν, κατέβαινε· καὶ τριταῖος ἀπὸ τῶν προειρημένων κρημνῶν διανύσας, ἥψατο τῶν ἐπιπέδων.

Hannibal, accompanied by his whole army, would have reached the plains *τριταῖος* from La Thuile, 77 M. P. above Ivrea; not his cavalry and infantry alone *ἑβδομαῖοι*. But there is another passage which shews that the part of Hannibal's army which first passed did not continue its march:

Τοῖς μὲν οὖν ὑποξυγίοις καὶ τοῖς ἵπποις ἱκανὴν ἐποίησε πάροδον ἐν ἡμέρᾳ μιᾷ. Διὸ καὶ ταῦτα μὲν εὐθέως διαγαγὼν καὶ καταστρατοπεδεύσας περὶ τοὺς ἐκφεύγοντας ἤδη τὴν χιόνα τόπους, διαφῆκε πρὸς τὰς νόμας.

It is obvious that when a body of men have encamped, and have turned their horses and other animals out to pasture, they cannot be at the same time on their march, as Messrs. W. and C. have assumed they might be. Yet the final assumption which must be made in order to save the theory of the Little St. Bernard is perhaps the strangest of all. Polybius says of Hannibal:

Τριταῖος ἀπὸ τῶν προειρημένων κρημνῶν διανύσας, ἥψατο τῶν ἐπιπέδων.

The distance from La Thuile to the commencement of the plains could therefore not be more than three days' march. Now how is *τριταῖος* to be converted into *ἑβδομαῖος*? I have already explained how *τριταῖος* is raised to *τεταρταῖος* by assuming three full days from Pré St. Didier, and therefore three and a-half from La Thuile. *Τεταρταῖος* is now to be raised to *ἑβδομαῖος*, by assuming, in the passage just cited, that the subjects of *διανύσας* and *ἥψατο* may be different, and that the passage may be interpreted thus:

Three clear days and a fraction (*τριταῖος* or, as

would be required, τεταρταῖος) after *Hannibal* had passed the precipices, *a part of his army, which had passed (as is assumed) three clear additional days before,* reached the plains.

This, it will be seen, must be the nature of the assumption made when we are told (p. 119):

"In point of fact the cavalry and infantry had six days (from Pré St. Didier) instead of three to perform this march in."

And also (p. 120):

"It is sufficient for our purpose to shew, that it was quite possible for the *main body of the army* to reach St. Martin without any difficulty," *i. e.* "on the third, or rather the fourth day, after *Hannibal* had passed the precipices."

Thus, if the cavalry and infantry, leaving La Thuile on the 12th day, reach the plains on the 18th, the word τριταῖος, which measures for Hannibal the intervening distance, is supposed to be satisfactorily explained. We must also change πεντεκαίδεκα into ὀκτωκαίδεκα, and even then leave the elephants behind; we must reject the words, συναθροίσας ὁμοῦ πᾶσαν τὴν δύναμιν; and we must assume that a body of men, who have encamped and turned their horses and beasts of burden out to pasture, are at the same time on their march with their horses. These are the expedients of Messrs. W. and C. to sustain the theory of the Little St. Bernard on one point alone, the distance of Hannibal's pass from the plains.

What I have said above on the arguments of Messrs. W. and C. may be a sufficient answer also to Mr. Law's way of obviating the objection (vol. I. p. 309):

"Polybius relates no such fact as the army getting in three days from the Little St. Bernard to the plains of Ivrea."

Yet $5-2=3$. "*Τριταῖος* signifies 'on the third day' of the
progress made on liberation of the elephants from the precipices, and is applied to the arrival of the head of the column
in the plain. It is consistent with the narrative that, when
this last event took place, the tail of the column of march was
between Aosta and Verres."

The third insuperable objection to the theory of
the Little St. Bernard is derived from the fact, that
Hannibal, as Polybius relates, pointed out to his
soldiers, from the summit of the pass which he crossed,
the plains of the Po, and indicated to them the position
of Rome. Now it is quite impossible to see any part
of the plain from the Little St. Bernard, as it would
also be from any of the mountains bordering on the
plateau which forms the summit of that pass. This
objection Messrs. W. and C. would obviate in the
following manner (p. 103):

"If any other passage commanded a view of the plains,
we might hesitate; but as none do"—this is not the case—
"we must content ourselves with explaining the account of
Polybius as well as we can. And if we confine ourselves to
the first part of his observations, we shall find nothing inconsistent with the state of the country on the Little St.
Bernard. Polybius says that Hannibal "endeavoured to
encourage his soldiers, having one resource for this, the sight
of Italy." Now that object was easily attainable from the
passage in question, as the valley of La Tuille is at the foot
of it, and would be perfectly visible," probably covered with
snow (p. 116), "from the pass itself by the whole army.
But when Polybius goes on to say that Hannibal *pointed out*
the plains of the Po, and explained the situation of Rome
itself, we must enlarge the expression so far as to suppose
that he called the stream which falls into the Po by the name
of that river, which he might as well do, as attempt to *point
out*"—here ἐνδείκνυμι and ὑποδείκνυμι are not distinguished:
see Dean Alford on Matt. IV. 8—"the situation of Rome

itself, and which, if correctly pointed out, would not have been very encouraging, as the passage"—*i. e.* of the Little St. Bernard (a strange reason this for impeaching the credit of Polybius!)—"is closed up by very high mountains on the S.E., and this is equally the case with the Mont Genèvre, which, like the Little St. Bernard, takes a N.E. direction from Savoy"—(Dauphiné)—"to Piedmont."—Of the route of the Mont Cenis, which takes a S.E. direction from Savoy to Piedmont, nothing is said.—"After all, the difficult expressions are nearly superfluous; for the mere fact of the descent of the waters on the side of the passage opposite to that by which the army had ascended, would sufficiently shew that the great difficulties were overcome, and there was time enough, during the two days' halt at the summit, to explain the fact of their having reached the highest point of the road."

I have now shewn how the theory of the Little St. Bernard fails when tested by the three great characteristics of the pass which Hannibal crossed: namely, that the Taurini should occupy the plains at its foot; that the summit of the pass should be not more than three of Hannibal's daily marches, or about 40 M. P., from the commencement of the plains; and that a view of those plains should be attainable from the summit. The concurrence of these three characteristics points to the Mont Cenis as Hannibal's route; and for the remainder of that route, or the part which would lie in Savoy or Dauphiné, there is nothing to give the Little St. Bernard the preference over the Mont Cenis, even if we admit the views of the Bernardine advocates with respect to it. Let them therefore be admitted, though I think them wrong, merely to abridge the argument.

The commencement of the Alpine route is fixed by Messrs. W. and C. at Le Chevelu, at the western foot of the Mont du Chat, which they consider (rightly) to be the Roman *Labisco*.   From here the distance to the commencement of the Italian plain ought to be about 1200 stadia, or 150 M. P.

By the Little St. Bernard, the Antonine Itinerary gives 176 M. P. between Labisco and Eporedia (*Ivrea*). The modern distance is 174 M. P.   By the high road of the Great Mont Cenis the distance would be:

	M. P.	
Labisco (*Le Chevelu*)		
Lemincum (*Chambéry*) .	14	(Ant. Itin.)
Segusio (*Susa*) .	113	(67½ Piedmontese miles).
Ad Fines (*Avigliana*) .	24	(Ant. Itin.)
	151	

and, by the Little Mont Cenis, about 144.

But, argue Messrs. W. and C. (p. 80), the Maurienne is "barren of all cultivation," so that "a large army, without magazines, must have been starved" (p. 89).   Yet Grillet, in his *Dictionnaire* (s. v. *Maurienne* and *Tarentaise*), besides allowing the Maurienne some cultivation, rather gives it the advantage over the Tarentaise, which leads to the Little St. Bernard.

To the Maurienne he allots, in Piedmontese *journaux* or acres—

En culture	242,041
En pâturages	178,601
En rochers, &c.	101,620
	522,262

and to the Tarentaise—

En culture	146,223
En pâturages	200,012
En rochers, &c.	99,388
	445,623

Another argument on the same side is (p. 80):

" Why should Hannibal, who was provided with guides, who must have known the *best* road,"—*i. e.* the Little St. Bernard—" have gone by the worst,"—*i. e.* the Mont Cenis—" even if it had been known at that time, while the *best* lay equally open to him ?"

The most proper answer to this is their own words (p. 194):

" The question to be discussed is, not which road was the *best*, or what was the shortest road from Spain to Italy, but what road Hannibal did himself take, as reported by the oldest historians."

But there is another answer.   No passage of historic note over the Alps has, so far as I am aware, been effected by the Little St. Bernard.   Pompey, Cæsar, Cæcina, Valens, Constantine, Charlemagne, and Napoleon, all preferred to pass by the Genèvre or Cenis, or the Great St. Bernard.   Why then are we to presume that Hannibal would have chosen to pass by the Little St. Bernard, even if it were the best road ?

From Le Chevelu to the summit of the Little St. Bernard the distance would be about 90 m. p., and to that of the Little Mont Cenis about 100.   Each would thus agree well enough with the fact, that Hannibal reached the summit of the Alps on the ninth day of his Alpine march.   There is also ample room for Hannibal to encamp, either on the summit of the Cenis or Little St. Bernard, as well as on the Genèvre. As to the *Leucopetron* of Polybius, which has been identified with the *Roche Blanche* in the Tarentaise, a precipice of white gypsum in which Dr. Arnold saw nothing conspicuous, about six miles from the summit of the Little St. Bernard, it may be sufficient to observe that such rocks are common in the Upper Maurienne.   " Vis-à-vis de cet endroit (a point a little below Lanslebourg)," writes De Saussure, "de l'autre côté de l'Arc, on voit des gypses blancs. Au reste, je n'ai point noté toutes les montagnes de ce genre de pierre que l'on rencontre sur cette route; elles y sont trop fréquemment répétées."[1]

Other arguments supposed to favour the theory of the Little St. Bernard I shall pass over still more rapidly: indeed, it is not easy to speak of some of them seriously. I shall, therefore, merely mention the buckler found at Passage in *the Island*, which Messrs. W. and C. (p. 57) consider to have been "very probably a votive tablet, placed in that spot either by Hannibal himself, or by some Carthaginian general, who followed him on that road with reinforcements." Nor shall I stay to consider the engineering or architectural works on the Little St. Bernard, which are attributed to Hannibal; especially as similar works are ascribed to him in several other parts of the Alps,[2] in pursuance of the great alternative principle of Alpine antiquarianism: *Aut Hannibal, aut diabolus.* I shall not even be induced to pause by the "very large bones of beasts," reported to have been found near the Roche Blanche; on which Messrs. W. and C. lay much stress (p. 94), and which may be sometimes heard of under the matured and imposing form of whole elephants, although it is to be feared that these attesting elephants have been lost or mislaid. Adequate justice has been done to such osteological evidence by two of our modern travellers, in reference to some similar fossil remains found in Tuscany; for the

---

[1] "Ecco, accanto ad un profondo burrone che l'Arco ha scavato in mezzo ai *bianchi calcari*, sorgere una fortezza. È questo il forte di Essillon."—*Bertolotti.* Yet I think *Leucopetron* means simply 'crag.' See Appendix.

[2] See Ladoucette, *Hautes Alpes*, pp. 55—59.

Little St. Bernard is not the only locality where a manufacture of Punic ivory has been established.[1]

Though I have admitted above, for the sake of abridging the argument, Messrs. W. and C.'s view of the occurrences on the western side of the pass of Hannibal, yet I really consider that view to be entirely wrong. The battle near the *Leucopetron* I believe must be identified with the 'great danger' which Polybius makes Hannibal to encounter on the fourth day of his Alpine march,[2] and I have no doubt that Hannibal approached the Alps along the left bank of the Isère, instead of adopting a circuit to cross mountains, δυσπρόσοδα καὶ δυσέμβολα, καὶ σχεδὸν, ὡς εἰπεῖν, ἀπρόσιτα.[3]

[1] "Large quantities of fossil bones have at various times been discovered in the valleys N. of Figline, near Levane and Montevarchi, and in the plain of Arezzo. The Italian antiquaries, ignorant of natural history, and eager to connect everything on this road with Hannibal, at once proclaimed them to be the bones of Hannibal's elephants. The fossil bones include those of the mastodon, hippopotamus, elephant, rhinoceros, hyæna, tiger, bear, and of several species of deer."—*Murray's Handbook for Central Italy*, p. 221, ed. 1853. This is a tolerably copious result from the single elephant which Hannibal brought into Etruria.

Mr. Weld, in his recent work on Florence (p. 297), also notices these fossil bones, and observes: "Historians, who frequently arrive at conclusions by no means borne out by facts, when they desire to support a favourite theory, were in the habit, before the lights of science burned as brightly as they do now, of pointing to these fossil remains as being those of the Carthaginian elephants which accompanied Hannibal in his famous expedition." He adds in a note: "Some fossil tusks suspended over one of the entrances to the cathedral of Arezzo, are believed by the inhabitants to be the tusks of Hannibal's elephants." It is noticed too in Murray (p. 127) that some fossil remains near the Metaurus are believed in like manner to be the relics of the army of Hasdrubal. A most amusing tradition about Hannibal may be found in a letter of Spence (Aug. 17, 1740).

[2] See my "summaries," *ante*, p. 22.

[3] See Appendix at the end on the route by the left bank of the Isère.

CHAPTER III.

THE first documents that I shall notice in connexion
with the Cottian tribes are two Inscriptions.   One is
that which still remains on the Arch of Susa, and is
dated in the year 8 B.C.   The other, which is preserved
by Pliny, was engraved on the Trophy of Augustus,
erected in the year 7 B.C. on the summit of the
Maritime Alp; a monument of which some remains
yet exist, and which has left its name to the modern
Turbia, overlooking the Mediterranean from the crest
of its lofty promontory, that rises from the sea to
a height of about 2000 feet.

These two inscriptions I shall speak of as the Inscription of Susa and the Inscription of Turbia.

The Inscription of Susa gives the names of the
Cottian ' civitates' in the following order:

Segovii, Segusini, Belaci, *Caturiges*, *Medulli*, Tebavii, *Adanates*, Savincates, *Egidinii* (or *Egdinii*),
Veaminii, Venicami, Imerii, *Vesubiani*, Quadiates.

The Inscription of Turbia enumerates the Alpine
tribes subdued by Augustus (Pliny, *H. N.* III. 24).
The names of the Rhætian tribes, which come first,
I omit, and commence with the Viberi at the source

of the Rhone. Proceeding from their name the inscription runs thus, with a comment of Pliny's at the end: .....Viberi, Nantuates, Seduni, Veragri, Salassi, Acitavones, *Medulli*, Uceni, *Caturiges*, Brigiani, Sogiontii, Brodiontii, Nemaloni, *Edenates*, *Esubiani*, *Veamini*, Gallitæ, Triulatti, *Ectini*, Vergunni, Eguituri, Nementuri, Oratelli, Nerusi, Velauni, Suetri. Non sunt adjectæ Cottianæ civitates XII, quæ non fuerunt hostiles : item attributæ municipiis Lege Pompeia.

The first thing to be observed in this last inscription, with reference to the names of the tribes whose position is known, beginning with the Viberi and ending with the Caturiges, is, that they are placed very nearly in order of contiguity or proximity. The Nantuates should indeed, in such a case, follow instead of preceding the Seduni; but that would be the only exception to the rule, the unknown Acitavones being in all probability identical with the missing Centrones, who ought to be in the list. I shall consequently, in determining the position of the remainder of the tribes mentioned, proceed on the supposition that a similar principle is adopted with them, or that they are named nearly in the same manner as the counties of England might be enumerated, if it were required to be done from memory, or by the aid of a map.

The next thing which requires notice is, that six of the fourteen Cottian tribes in the Inscription of Susa are found among the tribes conquered by Augustus; for I think that the identity of the *Adanates* and *Edenates*, of the *Vesubiani* and *Esubiani*, and of the *Egidinii* and *Ectini*, may be taken for granted. The remaining eight of the 'civitates' in the Inscription of Susa ought thus to be the same as the twelve

Cottian 'civitates' in the Inscription of Turbia, who were not hostile to the Romans and had received the *municipium* by the Pompeian Law. The discrepancy in point of number would probably be caused by four of the less important of the earlier Cottian communities being merged in some more important ones (as Strabo merges the Tricastini and Segalauni in the Cavares), and by the whole number of tribes being thus reduced from twelve to eight. These eight would occupy the original Cottian Land, and the remaining six of the Inscription of Susa would consist of tribes subdued by Augustus, and placed by him under the government of Cottius.

The original Cottian tribes would thus be these:

> Segovii,
> Segusini,
> Belaci,
> Tebavii,
> Savincates,
> Venicami,
> Imerii,
> Quadiates.

And the six tribes added by Augustus these:

> Caturiges,
> Medulli,
> Adanates,
> Ectini,
> Veamini,
> Vesubiani.

To determine the extent of the original Cottian Land it will be necessary first to determine the extent of the districts added to it. These will be found to consist of two; one occupied by the Caturiges and Medulli, and the other by the Adanates, Ectini,

Veamini, and Vesubiani. It is to these last four tribes that I shall now endeavour to assign their territory.

In the Inscription of Turbia the four following tribes are named in order:

Caturiges, Brigiani, Sogiontii, Brodiontii.

The Caturiges occupied Chorges (*Caturiges*) and Embrun (*Ebrodunum*), which Ptolemy makes their capital, with perhaps Gap (*Vapincum*) also: and the Brodiontii may be taken as identical with the Bodiontici of Pliny (III. 5), whose chief town was Digne (*Dinia*). In the river Bléone, on which Digne stands, the name of the Brodiontii may be preserved. The Brigiani and Sogiontii would probably occupy the vacant space between the Caturiges and the Brodiontii; the Sogiontii in the neighbourhood of Seyne, in which their name is perhaps found; and the Brigiani in the valley of Barcelonnette.

The line of nomenclature has hitherto proceeded from north to south, but now turns from west to east. Beginning with the Brodiontii, the next four tribes are:

Brodiontii, Nemaloni, Edenates, Esubiani;
the two latter being among the added Cottian tribes, and otherwise called Adanates and Vesubiani, which names I shall adopt.

As the Vesubiani may be fixed with confidence in the valley of the *Vesubia*, a tributary of the Var, the Nemaloni may be placed to the east of the Brodiontii, in the upper valley of the Verdon;[1] and the Adanates

---

[1] *Nem-* and *Nemet-*, which occur in the composition of so many Celtic names, as in the cases of the *Nem*-aloni and *Nem*-enturi in the Inscription of Turbia, are explained by Diefenbach (*Celtica*, I. 119) from the Gaelic *naomh*, 'holy.' *Nemet-* he interprets 'temple.' See also Zeuss, *Gram. Celt.*, p. 11. The names of *Allons* and *Allos*, two places in the upper

between the valleys of the Verdon and the Vesubia.
But before settling more nearly the position of the
Adanates, it will be better to proceed a little further
with the Inscription of Turbia.

After naming the Vesubiani, the line of nomenclature would have turned nearly west to the Vergunni,
whose name is found in the modern *Vergons*. From
the Nemaloni to the Vergunni the names are:

Nemaloni, Adanates, *Vesubiani*, Veamini, Gallitæ,
Triulatti, Ectini, *Vergunni*.

The five tribes of the Adanates, Veamini, Gallitæ,
Triulatti, and Ectini, would thus lie between the
Nemaloni and Vergunni on the west, and the Vesubiani on the east; and would also have been limited
on the south by the Nerusi, to whom Ptolemy assigns
the town of Vence (*Vintium*). Now the Vesubiani
were Cottian, and the town of Glandève (*Glannativa*)
is given in the *Notitia Provinciarum* to the province
of the Maritime Alps. The river Var, where it runs
from west to east, thus probably marked the boundary
between that district and the Cottian Land; and all
conditions will be satisfied if the Gallitæ and Triulatti,
who were not Cottian, be placed to the south of the
Var, and the Adanates, Ectini, and Veamini, to the
north of that river.

I have no clue to assign the position of the Veamini
more accurately: but the Ectini are usually placed in
the valley of the *Tinea*, on account of a certain resemblance between the two names; and Adanat(es) may
have become *Annot*, as Redones has become *Rennes*,
Atrebates *Arras*, Catalauni *Châlons*, Cadurci *Querci*,
Catoriges *Chorges*, and Bituriges *Berri* and *Bourges*.

---

valley of the Verdon, where the Nemaloni seem to have lived, have some
resemblance to the termination of that name.

Of the tribes named after the Vergunni I need not say much, as they have little concern with our subject. The Suetri are usually placed about Seillans, which is identified with their capital, *Salinœ*. The Velauni, whose name occurs between those of the Nerusi and Suetri, may be fixed about Grasse. The three remaining names, those of the Eguituri, Nementuri, and Oratelli, occur between those of the Vergunni and Nerusi, and are placed accordingly. There is some slight resemblance between the name of the Oratelli and that of the river *Artubie*. I may add that Cimiez (*Cemenelium*) near Nice belonged to the Vediantii and to the province of the Maritime Alps; Antibes (*Antipolis*) to the Deciates, Fréjus (Forum Julii) to the Oxybii, and Riez (*Reii*) to the Albiœci. These last three tribes were in the Narbonensian province, as was also the town of Gap. The Vocontii touched the Albiœci (Strabo, p. 203), and likewise, according to Ptolemy, the possessors of Digne, whom he calls Sentii; a name probably connected with the town of Senez (*Sanitium*), which he erroneously gives to the Vediantii. He may have made some confusion between Vediantii and Bodiontici.

The district occupied by four out of the six tribes added to the original Cottian tribes has now been determined. It remains to fix the position of the remaining two, the Caturiges and Medulli.

We should be inclined at first to identify the Cottian Caturiges with the Caturiges of Chorges and Embrun; but we find on enquiry that this district appears never to have been Cottian. I say nothing of the frontier of the Cottian Land being fixed by Strabo (p. 179) at Embrun, because he describes the Cottian Land before it received its additions. But

E

the Jerusalem Itinerary also fixes the commencement
of the *Alpes Cottiæ* at Embrun, which city the *Notitia
Provinciarum* makes the capital of the Maritime Alps:
and in an inscription found at Chorges (Ladoucette,
Hautes Alpes, p. 75), Annius Rufinus, Præfect of the
Maritime Alps, records his devotion to the Emperor
Nero. Pliny too (*H. N.* III. 24) speaks of Caturiges
(probably those of Chorges and Embrun) who were
not Cottian: "Sunt præterea Latio donati incolæ
(Alpium), ut Octodurenses [the Veragri, whose capital
was Octodurus, now Martigny], et finitimi Centrones,
Cottianæ civitates, Caturiges, et ex Caturigibus orti
Vagienni Ligures, et qui Montani dicuntur." This
passage shews, too, how the Caturiges were spread;
as does also another in Pliny (III. 21): "Interiere et
Caturiges Insubrum exsules." It may be added that
there was a place called Caturiges or Caturigis at or
near Bar-le-Duc in Lorraine.[1]

Laying aside for a time the question of the Caturiges, I turn to consider the position of the sixth of
the added Cottian tribes, the Medulli. They are
rightly placed by D'Anville in the Lower Maurienne,
or valley of the Arc, in Savoy: but I will nevertheless
give the reasons why they should be fixed there, as
their position is of great importance.

Along the Rhone, from the Durance to the Isère,
Strabo places the Cavares, among whom he therefore
includes the Segalauni or Segovellauni (Valence) of
Pliny and Ptolemy, and also the Tricastini. In one
passage Ptolemy fixes these last east of the Segalauni,
and touching the Allobroges: in another, he makes

---

[1] Zeuss connects the name Caturiges with the Gaelic *cath*, 'battle.'
I should be inclined to prefer *cadha*, 'a narrow pass,' = English *gate*,
'porta.' It would explain better the name of a mountain people.

them touch the Memini, to whom Pliny gives Car-
pentras, and whom Ptolemy makes (with the Vocontii)
to lie to the west of the possessors of Digne. These
two contacts of the Tricastini, with the Allobroges
and the Memini, can hardly be reconciled together,
and the probability is that the Tricastini lay, according to the general opinion, only to the south, and not
to the east, of the Segalauni.

Beyond the Cavares, Strabo places the Vocontii,
Tricorii, Iconii, and Medulli (p. 185). The Vocontii,
to whom Pliny gives Vaison and Die, extended, according to Strabo (p. 178), as far as Embrun, where
they touched the Cottian Land. They also (p. 203)
touched the Allobroges; a contact which must be
fixed not far from Grenoble, since the Segalauni, if
not also the Tricastini, occupied the left bank of the
Isère more to the west, in the neighbouring district
of the Valentinois. As the Cottian Land began at
Embrun, all the valley of the Durance above Embrun
would have been Cottian, and the western boundary
of that territory would have been formed here by the
great ridge of the Alps of Dauphiné, which culminates
in the Mont Pelvoux.

Proceeding with Strabo, we find (p. 203) that he
notices the Iconii and Tricorii as lying beyond the
Vocontii, and the Medulli as lying beyond the Iconii
and Tricorii. The Iconii and Tricorii would thus be
situated to the west of the Pelvoux ridge, and to the
north-east of a line (not necessarily straight) drawn
from near Embrun to near Grenoble. This fixes these
two tribes in the Pays d'Oysans and its neighbourhood, and identifies the Iconii of Strabo with the Uceni
of the Inscription of Turbia, whose name is found in
Oysans or Oisans. Compare the French *oiseau* with

the Italian *uccello*. Strabo's Medulli, whom he places beyond, or to the north-east of the Iconii and Tricorii, would thus be found in the Lower Maurienne.

Again. The Medulli lie (Strabo, p. 204) on one side of a mountain chain; and on the other side, which slopes towards Italy, lie the Taurini and other Ligurians, including the Cottians, of whom we know the Segusini to have formed a part. This brings the Medulli into the Maurienne.

Next to the Taurini, says Strabo (p. 204), come the Salassi; and in the mountains above the Salassi lie the Centrones and Catoriges and Veragri (Martigny) and Nantuates (between the Veragri and the Lake of Geneva, and extending, as we know from Cæsar, to the Allobroges). There is nothing in this about the Medulli; but the account of Strabo, beginning with the Vocontii and ending here, is to be considered as exhaustive, and therefore either his Centrones (Tarentaise) or Catoriges, or else both of them, would intervene between the Medulli and the Salassi.

Thus far from Strabo. Further confirmation of the position assigned to the Medulli may be found in Ptolemy (II. 10), who makes them border on the Allobroges; and also in the Inscription of Turbia, which gives the following sequence of tribes: Veragri, Salassi, Acitavones (= Centrones), Medulli, Uceni. Another fact may be mentioned concerning the Medulli. They were subject to *goître*, as appears from a passage in Vitruvius quoted by Cluverius in his *Italy* (p. 773): "Æquiculis in Italia et in Alpibus natione Medullorum est genus aquæ, quam qui bibunt, efficiuntur turgidis gutturibus." The injurious quality of the water would be an inference from the existence of *goître*. On this passage of Vitruvius a commentator of the sixteenth century (Philander, in Varior. Ed., Amst. 1649) observes: "Videtur intelligere habitatores vallis Cilleræ (Zillerthal in Tyrol), quæ distat ab Oeno octavum lapidem, meridiem versus; iis enim aquarum vitio guttur intumescit. Turget et iis qui *vallem Morianam* ad Alpes Cottias incolunt, sed maxime qui ab Aquabella (Aiguebelle) Cameram (La Chambre) usque dextra habitant, nempe quibus non rara propendula gutturis struma in humerum rejicitur." The Lower Maurienne, indeed, is notorious for this malady.

It may have been observed that Strabo, in one of the passages cited above, mentions the name of the last of the six tribes added to the Cottian state, the Caturiges or Catoriges. In the mountains above the Salassi, he says, are the Centrones and Catoriges and Veragri and Nantuates. Where then should these Catoriges be placed? Not on the east of the Centrones, for there were the Salassi; nor with any probability on the north, for the Veragri touched the Centrones—Octodurenses et finitimi Centrones (Pliny, III. 24); nor yet on the west, where the Medulli and Allobroges would have been. The Catoriges thus seem to have lain on the south of the Centrones, that is to say, in the Upper Maurienne.

There are only two objections, as far as I am aware, to this supposition. Strabo, as will be seen presently, seems to extend the Medulli to the pass of the Mont Cenis, and takes no notice of the Caturiges of Chorges, unless they are mentioned here as the Catoriges. But it may be doubted whether a geographer like Strabo could make such an error as to speak of the Centrones, the people of Chorges, the Veragri, and the Nantuates as occupying the mountains above the Salassi. It is at least possible, to say no more, that he may have been right, and that there may consequently have been Catoriges in the Upper Maurienne, especially as the name often recurs.

In either case, whether the Medulli occupied the whole of the Maurienne or shared it with the Catoriges, that district would have formed one of those added to the original Cottian Land; and the country of Chorges, if ever added to that territory (which I do not think), would only have been a temporary acquisition. And thus the actual acquisitions made by the Cottian state would have consisted of two districts, divided from the original territory by the main chain of the Alps; of the Maurienne, beyond the Mont Cenis, on the north; and of the high mountains drained by the Var and its tributaries on the south.

The original Cottian Land is thus found to comprise the Italian valleys between the Mont Cenis and the main chain of the Maritime Alps dividing France from Italy; and also, on the French side of the Mont Genèvre, all the valley of the Durance above Embrun. And this extent of territory was occupied by the eight tribes who are named in the following order in the Inscription of Susa:

Segovii, Segusini, Belaci, Tebavii, Savincates, Venicami, Imerii, Quadiates.

Only two of these tribes can be placed with confidence, the Segusini and the Quadiates. The position of the first is marked by Susa (*Segusio*), and that of the last by St. Martin de *Queyrières* in the valley of the Durance, and *Queyras* in the tributary valley of the Guil. These names are still more like *Quariates*, a tribe mentioned by Pliny (III. 5) in the following connexion: "Regio, Oxubiorum, Ligaunorumque:

super quos Suetri, Quariates, Adunicates (probably=
Adanates)." The question arises, Were the Quadiates
and Quariates identical? Against their identity it
may be urged, that the Quariates seem placed more to
the south than the Quadiates could have been: but
this is met by the stronger argument, that the Quariates, lying north of the Oxybii, and probably of the
Suetri as well, would either have been among the
tribes subdued by Augustus, or else one of the original
Cottian tribes. But their name is not found in the
Inscription of Turbia, and therefore they were probably Cottian; in which case we can hardly avoid
considering them the same as the Quadiates.

To the Segusini, then, we must give the valley of
Susa, or of the Dora; and to the Quadiates or Quariates the Cottian part of the valley of the Durance.
For the remaining six tribes, the Segovii, Belaci,
Tebavii, Savincates, Venicami, and Imerii, there consequently remain the six Italian valleys of the Clusone,
Pelice, Po, Varaita, Maira, and Stura. Each tribe
may be supposed to have possessed one valley, though
we cannot determine how they were distributed, as
the order of the tribes in the Inscription of Susa
seems to be according to no rule, and there are no
particular resemblances of names.[1]

Having thus defined the territory of the original
Cottian tribes, I have next to notice the first event
known in their history. After enumerating, from the

---

[1] The only resemblances which I have traced (and these are but slight)
are between the Venicami and *Vinadio*, the chief place in the valley of the
Stura; and between the Imerii and Belaci and the rivers *Maira* and
Pelice. Perhaps the Segovii occupied the valley of the Clusone; the
Belaci, that of the Pelice; the Tebavii, that of the Po; the Savincates,
that of the Varaita; the Imerii, that of the Maira; and the Venicami,
that of the Stura. I speak, of course, of the *southern* Stura.

Inscription of Turbia, the Alpine tribes subdued by Augustus, Pliny adds :

Non sunt adjectæ Cottianæ civitates XII, quæ non fuerunt hostiles; item attributæ municipiis Lege Pompeia.

This *Lex Pompeia* was the law, carried B.C. 89 by Pompeius Strabo, the father of Pompey the Great, which gave the *Jus Latii* to the Transpadane communities (Smith, *Dict. Antiq.* s. v. LEX POMPEIA). The original Cottian tribes, as we see, received the franchise at the same time as Transpadane Gaul, and would thus have been connected with Rome from the year 89 B.C. As I shall have nothing more to do with the additions to the Cottian Land, I shall for the future speak of these original tribes as simply the Cottian tribes. The Cottian Land, therefore, with which we shall have to deal, is the territory inclosed in the map by a red line. This territory, from the year 89 B.C., would be in a state of amity and alliance with Rome, if not in a state of dependence upon the greater power.

I have now given my reasons for placing the various tribes as I have done on the map, and have been particularly full on the position of the Medulli, as it is of great importance in the present investigation. For the next question I shall have to consider is, the pass alluded to by Strabo between the country of the Medulli and Italy.

The mountains of the Medulli, he tells us (p. 203), are so high, as to be said to require an ascent of 100 stadia, with a descent of equal length to the frontiers of Italy (σταδίων ἑκατὸν ἔχειν φασὶ τὴν ἀνάβασιν καντεῦθεν πάλιν τὴν ἐπὶ τοὺς ὄρους τοὺς τῆς Ἰταλίας κατάβασιν). I might, I think, take for granted, that an ἀνάβασις on one side of a mountain, and a κατάβασις on the other, are equivalent to a ὑπέρβασις, or pass: but I will, nevertheless, cite some passages in illustration of the use of the word ἀνάβασις.

The acropolis of Corinth, about 2000 feet in height, is thus described by Strabo (p. 379):

Ὄρος ὑψηλὸν ὅσον τριῶν ἥμισυ σταδίων ἔχον τὴν κά-
θετον, τὴν δ᾽ ἀνάβασιν καὶ τριάκοντα σταδίων.

The perpendicular height was $3\frac{1}{2}$ stadia (about 2100 feet), and *the length of the way up* 30 stadia (about $3\frac{1}{2}$ miles). He says likewise (p. 223) of Volterra (about 1900 feet above the sea):

Ἡ δ᾽ ἐπ᾽ αὐτὴν ἀνάβασις πεντεκαίδεκα σταδίων ἐστὶν
ἀπὸ τῆς βάσεως, ὀξεῖα πᾶσα καὶ χαλεπή.

The *way up* was steep and difficult, and 15 stadia (about $1\frac{3}{4}$ miles) in length.

I may also cite, from Polybius, two other instances. He speaks (v. 44) of the ridge of Zagros, τὸ Ζάγρον ὄρος, ὃ τὴν μὲν ἀνάβασιν ἔχει πρὸς ἑκατὸν στάδια, the exact measurement given by Strabo in speaking of the Alpine chain between the Medulli and Italy. But I suppose there is little doubt that Polybius is speaking here of the pass of Zagros, τῆς τοῦ Ζάγρου ὑπερθέσεως, ἥπερ καλεῖται Μηδικὴ πύλη (Strabo, p. 525). This pass, now the pass of Kerrend, is described in Southgate's *Armenian and Persian Travels* (vol. ii. p. 335). He gives the day's journey across it from Kerrend to Serpoul at 10 hours, or 30 miles, and notices elsewhere (p. 143) that the pass terminates 2 hours before reaching Serpoul. Thus the whole length of the pass would be 8 hours, 24 miles, or about 200 stadia: and if the eastern and western ascents were of the same length, either would give the 100 stadia which Polybius assigns to the ἀνάβασις of Zagros.

The other instance from Polybius is this. In describing (x. 30) the passage of Mount Labus, between Parthia and Hyrcania, by king Antiochus, he says:

Ἦν γὰρ τὸ μὲν ὅλον μῆκος τῆς ἀναβάσεως περὶ τριακοσίους σταδίους.

The whole length of the ascent, *i. e.* the length of the way through the mountains up to the foot of the ridge to be crossed, added to the subsequent ascent of that ridge itself, was about 300 stadia. Thus the ἀνάβασις of the actual Mont Cenis, *i. e.* from Susa, is 100 stadia, like the pass of Zagros; while τὸ ὅλον μῆκος τῆς ἀναβάσεως from the Italian plain, *i. e.* from Avigliana, is 300 stadia, like the pass of Labus.

I cannot see how, when the height of a mountain, or of a mountain-chain, is estimated by the length of its ἀνάβασις, anything else can be indicated than the length of the way up to the summit; and I consequently infer that there was an ancient way up from the Maurienne to the summit of the ridge dividing it from Italy, and also a way thence down into Italy. Strabo is speaking of a ὑπέρβασις, and divides it into its ἀνάβασις and κατάβασις. Besides, it is not likely that the ancients would have known any Alpine ascents but those of the passes.

What was this pass? It might possibly be allowable to assume at once that it was the Mont Cenis, the only great pass between the Maurienne and Italy. But it may be better to enter into the question more particularly. A descent of 100 stadia, or nearly 12 English miles, led from the summit of the pass to the frontier of Italy; a frontier which the Jerusalem

Itinerary fixes at Susa: "inde incipit Italia."[1] The
summit of Strabo's pass, we may thus infer, was about
12 miles from Susa, and also 12 miles from the main
valley of the Maurienne.

Now there are three passes leading from Susa into
the Maurienne; the Col de Clairée, the Little Mont
Cenis, and the Great Mont Cenis. The pass of the
Clairée leads from Susa to Bramans in the valley of
the Arc, and the pass of the Great Mont Cenis from
Susa to Lanslebourg. The Little Mont Cenis lies
between the two. It ascends from Susa by the same
road as the Great Mont Cenis to the commencement
of the plateau of the Mont Cenis at La Grande Croix;
crosses that plateau by a path of its own to the Col of
the Little Mont Cenis; and falls, about five minutes'
walk beyond it, into the path from the Col de Clairée,
which it follows to Bramans.

I crossed the Col de Clairée in the year 1850.
Its summit is about 12 miles from Susa, and also
from Bramans; and the pass commands, as may be
known even from our handbooks, a noble view of
the plains of Italy up to the Apennines. I cannot
say whether this view is visible from the actual
summit, for I had to pass through a cloud there;
but I well remember the view opening upon me as
I emerged from the mist: it might have tempted
me to bring Hannibal over here, when I was led to
devote my attention to the subject of his passage of
the Alps, had I not found afterwards that a similar
but much inferior view might be obtained from the

---

[1] I cannot now assume, what I shall afterwards prove, that Scingomagus, where Strabo makes Italy begin, was the same as Susa. Yet
I will observe here that he places Scingomagus 71 m. p. from Embrun,
reckoned over the Mont Genèvre, and that this is the distance from
Embrun to Susa.

Mont Cenis. Yet, though the Clairée deserves to
be mentioned, I do not think it is likely to have
been the ancient road from the Maurienne to Susa.
It has a much more difficult descent into Italy than
the Little Mont Cenis, and its summit is about 1000
feet higher. The path also from the Clairée, on the
northern side of the pass, after having descended for
about five miles, passes within five minutes' walk of
the Col of the Little Mont Cenis: so that, upon the
whole, the latter route is far more likely to have
been taken.

The length of the modern high road over the
Great Mont Cenis, with its numerous zigzags, is
given in the *Guide à Suse et au passage du Grand
Mont Cenis*, at 37081 mètres = 23 miles. But the
old road was about 4 miles shorter. The distance
from Susa to La Grande Croix is about 11 miles;
the length of the plateau, 5 miles; and the descent
to Lanslebourg, 3 miles. The ascent from Lanslebourg to the summit of the Great Mont Cenis could
not thus be given at 100 stadia, which would bring
us 3 or 4 miles down the descent on the Italian side
from the southern edge of the plateau.

By the Little Mont Cenis the distances are nearly
these: from Bramans to the Col, 7 miles; across the
plateau to La Grande Croix, 6 miles; to Susa, 11
miles. If we measure 12 miles either from Susa
or Bramans, we shall thus be brought to the point,
about a mile north-west of La Grande Croix, where
the route crosses a ridge of hills on the plateau,
which extend from the lake till their southern extremity forms part of the brow of the abrupt declivity
of the mountain on the Italian side. It is from the
most southern of this range of hills, the Hauteur du

Combet, that the plains of Italy and the Apennines are seen.

The Little Mont Cenis has thus, I think, the best claim to be chosen as the ancient road between the Maurienne and Susa. Some slight confirmation of this may be derived from the circumstance that the Little Mont Cenis was called the Roman Road three centuries ago : " Cinesium minorem, qui Italice Strata Romana dicitur."[1] The circumstance that the Mont Cenis bore the title of the Roman Road is also noticed by Bergier (A.D. 1622) in his *Histoire des Grand Chemins de l' Empire* (p. 444) : but he is unaware that there were two passes over the Mont Cenis, and is certainly wrong in supposing that the road over that mountain was made by Pompey : " Les Romains," he says, " ont donné a ce chemin le nom de *Strada Romana*, comme si par dessus tous les autres, cetuy-cy estoit propre aux Romains, estant fait par l' un de leurs Capitaines généraux (*i. e.*, Pompey): ou bien si c' estoit le plus facile pour aller des Gaules en la ville de Rome." Simler (p. 95) agrees with Bergier in supposing that Hannibal

---

[1] Simler, *de Alpibus Commentarius*, p. 95 (A.D. 1574). As Simler, however, makes errors which may be thought to invalidate his testimony, I will cite what he says on the question whether the Mont Cenis was Graian or Cottian. I need hardly point out his errors, for they are too glaring not to be noticed. "Cum autem duo sunt juga montis Cinesii, equidem si de altiore (?) loquantur, quod Salassis propius est et ad Centrones (?) ducit, ferri utcunque potest eorum opinio, cum hoc jugum videri possit pars quædam Graiarum Alpium : sed si Cinesium minorem intelligunt, qui Italice Strata Romana dicitur, minus probari potest eorum sententia, cum iter hoc recte a Segusio incipiens, potius Cottiis Alpibus adnumerari debeat." And again (p. 94) : "Verum prope hoc jugum [Little St. Bernard] aliæ sunt Alpes, quas Montem Cales [Galèse] et Cinisium majorem nominant, per utrasque ad Centrones itur, a Tanrinis recto itinere, juxta Sturam fluvium." The Galèse is reached by the Orco, and the Cenis by the Dora, and neither by the intermediate Stura.

crossed the Great St. Bernard, and in the opinion
that the Mont Cenis was the more convenient road
into Spain opened by Pompey: "illud enim iter
multo opportunius est Penninis Alpibus, per quas
Hannibal transivisse creditur: ac *hodie* propterea
quod omnium usitatissimum sit ex Hispania et Gallia
et Britannia Romam euntibus, *Strata Romana* ab
Italis dicitur."

This last reason for the name might apply very
well to the route of the Great Mont Cenis; but it
cannot explain why the Little Mont Cenis should
have borne the title of the Roman Road. If it did
bear that name in Simler's time, the simplest explanation would be the best. The Little Mont Cenis
was the ancient Roman road across the mountain,
and it retained that name in modern times as a dis-
tinction from the Great Mont Cenis, which was the
new line of way. It is thus we should interpret
such a name among ourselves, as in the Lay of the
Last Minstrel:

> "Broad on the left before him lay,
> For many a mile, the Roman way."

This ancient road, commemorated by Sir Walter
Scott, is still called the "Street," by which, or some
similar name, so many stations on Roman roads are
indicated among us. I find in Majer's map of Savoy
(A.D. 1749) a place called St. Pierre de *Stratane*
between the Col of the Little Mont Cenis and Bramans.[1]

---

[1] Grillet, in his *Dictionnaire des départemens du Mont Blanc et du
Léman*, speaks of a Roman road as existing on the Mont Cenis (s. v.);
but I never remarked any decided traces of it: "Les itinéraires Romains
n'indiquant aucune voie militaire à travers le Mont-Cenis, on a lieu
de présumer que celle qui y existe aujourd'hui (1807) ne fut pratiquée
que sur les derniers tems de la république." This argument is bad, as
the Roman Itineraries belong to the Imperial times.

I now return for a short time to Strabo, and proceed with his account from where I left it off. After
having spoken of the mountains of the Medulli as
requiring an ascent of 100 stadia, succeeded by a
descent of the same length to the frontiers of Italy, he
says: that a great lake is found above in a hollow in
the mountains, and that there are two sources not far
from one another: from one of these sources proceeds
the Durance and the Dora of the Salassi (Segusini),
and from the other the Po. The 'great lake' can be
no other than the lake of the Mont Cenis, which was
thus described in a letter by Gray, when he crossed
the Mont Cenis into Italy on the 6th of November,
1739, about ten days later in the year than when
Hannibal encamped on the summit of the Alps: "It
was six miles to the top,[1] where a plain opens itself
about as many more in breadth, covered perpetually
(?) with very deep snow, and in the midst of that
a great lake of unfathomable depth, from which a
river takes its rise, and tumbles over monstrous rocks
quite down the other side of the mountain. The
descent is six miles more, but infinitely more steep
than the going up." The source from which the
Durance and the Dora (not of the Salassi, but the
Segusini) rise, would be the summit of the Mont
Genèvre, and the other source, from which the Po
rises, of course the eastern foot of the Viso.

It is just possible, as this description is rather
confused and incorrect, and is, besides, subjoined to
Strabo's notice of the pass into Italy, that it may be
said that he intended to point out the Mont Genèvre
as the pass in question. Let us see, therefore, how

---

[1] Keysler more correctly makes it one league, requiring "a full hour
of climbing up," *i. e.* from Lanslebourg.

the question lies. The western foot of the Genèvre is
at Briançon (*Brigantio*) in the valley of the Durance,
and its eastern foot at Cesanne (*Gesdao*) in the valley
of the Dora. Between these two places the Roman
Itineraries rightly give a distance of 10 M. P., divided
in one instance into 6 + 5. The ἀνάβασις and κατάβασις of the Genèvre were consequently each about
40 stadia in length, instead of 100.

But it might be urged, that we ought to measure
the κατάβασις, as Strabo does, to the frontier of Italy.
Now that frontier is made by Strabo (p. 179) to be 71
M. P., from Embrun, reckoned over the Mont Genèvre,
which the Itineraries correctly place at about 40 M. P.
from Embrun. The distance from the summit of the
Genèvre to Strabo's Italian frontier was therefore
about 30 M. P., or 240 stadia instead of 100. The
Mont Genèvre, again, cannot agree with what follows
in Strabo (p. 204), when he returns from his digres-
sion to the Medulli. "Now the Medulli," he proceeds, "lie above (ὑπέρκεινται μάλιστα—μήκιστα has
been suggested) the confluence of the Rhone and
Isère; and upon the opposite side of the aforesaid
chain, which slopes towards Italy, dwell the Taurini
and other Ligurians, of whose country what is called
the land of Ideonnus (= Donnus the father of Cottius)
and of Cottius forms a part." But the chain of the
Genèvre lay entirely within the Cottian Land, and
could have formed no line of demarcation between the
Medulli and the Ligurians.

This chapter may be concluded with a word or two
on the manner in which it bears upon the question of
Hannibal's passage of the Alps. Only two names of
peoples are mentioned by Polybius in his account of
that passage; the Allobroges and the Taurini. Han-

nibal's route lay from one of these nations to the
other, through Alpine tribes left without a name by
the historian. Now we learn from Ptolemy that the
Allobroges bordered on the Medulli, and we gather
from Strabo that a pass (the Little Mont Cenis) led
from the country of the Medulli to that of the Taurini.
The route which I have marked out for Hannibal
over the Little Mont Cenis is therefore satisfactory in
these respects. It agrees also very well with the
approach to the Alps indicated by Livy, from the
Tricastini *per extremam oram Vocontiorum in Tricorios*,
but not with his subsequent mention of the Durance ;
in which direction, however, it is quite certain that
Hannibal would find no Allobroges to attack him, as
Polybius says they did, about 100 M. P. from the confluence of the Rhone and Isère.

Messrs. Wickham and Cramer fix the Medulli, in
their map, on the mountains between the Maurienne
and Grenoble.[1] Mr. Law leaves no inhabitants at all
in the Maurienne, removing the Medulli to the summit
of the main chain of the Alps by the Little St. Bernard,
and enclosing them between the Salassi and the Centrones. As a sanitary measure for the relief of *goître*,
this change of air would be the most effective ex-
pedient to adopt ; though it may be less successful in
inducing the reader to accept the Little St. Bernard,
instead of the Little Mont Cenis, as Strabo's pass
between the Medulli and the Ligurians.

---

[1] In their text, however (p. 180), they correctly speak of the Maurienne
as being occupied by the Medulli, or Garoceli ; though they have not
perceived the identity of these two tribes.

CHAPTER IV.

THE POSITIONS OF OCELUM AND SCINGOMAGUS DETERMINED.

THERE are four conditions for the determination of the position of Ocelum, and four also for the determination of that of Scingomagus.

Ocelum lay $\begin{cases} \text{1. On the side of the Dora.} \\ \text{2. On the Cottian frontier, but in the Roman} \\ \qquad \text{province.} \\ \text{3. At the commencement of the Alps.} \\ \text{4. 99 M. P. from Embrun by the Mont Genèvre.} \end{cases}$

These conditions may be thus proved:

1. According to Strabo (p. 217) the direct way from Placentia to Ocelum on the Cottian frontier ran along the rivers Po and Dora (παρὰ τὸν Πάδον καὶ τὸν Δουρίαν ποταμόν); the Dora Susina, not the Dora Baltea, being plainly meant, for no road to the Cottian frontier could have run by the side of the Dora Baltea. As the Po would have been first followed by a road from the east, Ocelum would be found by the Dora, the second of the two rivers named.

2. Strabo, p. 217, p. 179. Cæsar, B. G. lib. i. cap. 10.

3. Strabo, p. 217: Ἐντεῦθεν δὲ ἤδη τὰ Ἄλπεια ὄρη καὶ ἡ Κελτική.

4. Strabo, p. 179. It may be as well to shew that Strabo's numbers here are correct. From Tarascon to the Vocontian frontier he gives 63 M. P.; thence

to Embrun, the Vocontian and Cottian frontier, 99
M. P.; and thence to Ocelum *as many more.* It is not
known where the first Vocontian frontier was: but
the whole distance from Tarascon to Embrun, 63 + 99
= 162 M. P., is certainly correct; for it is, as it ought
to be, 7 or 8 M. P. less than the distance from Embrun
to Arles in the Antonine Itinerary. The length of
the modern road from Tarascon to Embrun is 259 kilomètres, = 174 M. P., or 12 M. P. more than what
Strabo gives. But the ancient road was rather more
direct, especially between Cavaillon (*Cabellio*) and Apt
(*Apta Julia*). Here the straight distance is 25 M. P.;
the ancient distance, 28 M. P.; and the modern distance, 51 kilomètres, = 34 M. P.

As the total of Strabo's two distances is thus
correct, we must either assume that each one of them
is so, or that the error of one in excess is exactly
equal to the error of the other in defect; a supposition
extremely improbable. We may therefore conclude
that there were really 63 miles from Tarascon to the
Vocontian frontier, 99 M. P. thence to Embrun, and
consequently 99 M. P. from Embrun to Ocelum. Strabo
has fortunately expressed the distance between Embrun
and Ocelum in such a manner as to remove all probability of error.

Now the ancient itineraries make the distance
from Embrun to Susa, by the Mont Genèvre, to vary
between 70 and 72 M. P., and that from Susa to Ad
Fines, the Cottian frontier between Susa and Turin,
to lie between 22 and 24 M. P. Ad Fines would consequently be from 92 to 96 M. P. from Embrun; and
as it lies by the Dora, on the Cottian frontier, and
also where the Alps and the plain meet, it is clear
that it must have been very near Ocelum. Sickler,

indeed, in Ersch and Gruber's Encyclopædia, identifies Ocelum with Avigliana, as also does Mannert: but, since Ocelum was 99 M. P. from Embrun, and Ad Fines (*Avigliana*) not more than 96 at most, Ocelum should be a little further to the east. I find in Raymond's map a hamlet called *Urtiola*, 3 M. P. from Avigliana, near Buttigliera. This would occupy the position required for Ocelum, of which name its own might not impossibly be a corruption.

The four conditions for the determination of the position of Scingomagus are these:

Scingomagus lay
1. 519 M. P., or 4152 stadia, from Rome.
2. 71 M. P. from Embrun.
3. At the foot of the Alps.
4. Where Italy began.

These conditions are thus deduced:

1. Pliny, *H. N.* lib. ii. c. 112. Agathemerus, p. 11, in Hudson, *Geogr. Græc. Minor.* vol. ii.

2. Strabo, p. 179, makes Ocelum 99 M. P. from Embrun, and Scingomagus 28 M. P. above Ocelum. The difference is 71 M. P.

3. Agathemerus, p. 11. Ἀπὸ Ῥώμης ἐπὶ τὰς Ἄλπεις ἕως Σκιγγομάγου κώμης ὑπὸ ταῖς Ἄλπεσιν οὔσης στάδια δρνβ'.

4. Strabo, p. 179: ἡ ἀπὸ Σκιγγομάγου δὲ ἤδη Ἰταλία λέγεται.

All these conditions are satisfied by Susa.

1. Susa was about 519 M. P. from Rome.

The road from Rome to Susa would have run in the first instance to Genoa by the Aurelian Way.

We have three authorities to aid us in determining the distance between Rome and Genoa: Pliny, Strabo, and the Antonine Itinerary. I shall take these in the order in which they are named.

The coast of Liguria, Pliny says (III. 7), extends 211 M. P. between the Var and the Magra; and the Tiber (III. 8) is 284 M. P. from the Magra.   Pliny reckons, as appears from his mention of Fregenæ, to the mouth of the Tiber, and not to Rome; but as the Ant. Itin. makes both Rome and the Portus to be 34 M. P. from Pyrgi, the distances would be the same, whether reckoned to Rome or the mouth of the Tiber.

The distance from Rome to the Var was consequently $284 + 211 = 495$ M. P.; from which we have to subtract the distance between Genoa and the Var, in order to determine the distance between Rome and Genoa.

Now the distance between Genoa and the Var seems capable of being accurately computed.   Strabo gives 260 stadia, $= 32\frac{1}{2}$ M. P., between Genoa and Vado (*Vada Sabata*), which is confirmed by the modern distance of 35 M. P., and the distance of 30 M. P. in the Maritime Itinerary.   Next comes Albenga, which, by the modern road, is 29 M. P. from Vado.   The Peut. Tab. gives also 29 M. P.; and the Ant. Itin. XII + VIII $= 20$, or, according to another and better reading, XII + XVIIII, $= 31$ M.P.   Taking the true distance at $29\frac{1}{2}$ M. P., Albenga would be 62 M. P. from Genoa.

From Albenga to the Var, the Ant. Itin. would be correct throughout.   It gives us $XV + XVI + XVI = 47$ M. P. to Ventimiglia, instead of the modern distance of 50 M. P.; and $X + VI + VIIII + VI = 31$ M. P. to the Var, instead of the modern distance of 35 M. P.[1]

[1] Several Roman milestones have been found between Ventimiglia and the Var (Bertolotti, *Viaggio nella Liguria Marittima*, Lettera xvi.), and shew that Ventimiglia was, by the Æmilian Way, 590 M. P. from Rome; and the Var 621.   As these distances are thus reckoned through Rimini and Placentia, they are of little or no service here.   Yet as they help to confirm some of the distances in the text, as well as some others

Strabo gives (p. 202) 480 stadia from Albenga to Monaco, and rather more than 200 from Monaco to Antibes, which he makes (p. 184) to be about 60 stadia beyond the Var, though the Ant. Itin. makes this last distance more correctly to be 10 M. P., $= 80$ stadia. Thus Strabo makes rather more than $480 + 200 - 60 = 620$ stadia, $= 77\frac{1}{2}$ M. P. between Albenga and the Var; while the Ant. Itin., as above, makes the distance $47 + 31 = 78$ M. P. This is a very close agreement.

which I shall afterwards use, I will shew how the distance of 621 M. P. from Rome to the Var is made up.

The total distance from Rome to Milan is given in the Ant. Itin. (ed. Parthey and Pinder, p. 57) at 433 M. P., and the distance from Placentia to Milan at 40 M. P. The distance from Rome to Placentia was therefore 393 M. P., which is closely confirmed in the following manner:

	M. P.	
Rome		
Ocriculum	. .	45 (Ant. Itin., 24 + 21).
Ariminum	. .	169 (1350 stadia, Strabo, p. 227).
Placentia	. .	177 (Ant. Itin. by summation).

391

We may therefore assume the distance from Rome to Placentia to be 392 M. P.; a conclusion which I shall employ subsequently. From Placentia to Dertona the Ant. Itin. gives correctly $25 + 16 + 10 = 51$ M. P.; another distance which will also enter into a future calculation. And the whole distance of 621 M. P. to the Var will be thus completed from the Ant. Itin.:

				M. P.	
Roma					
Placentia .	.	.	.	CCCXCII	
Dertona .	.	.	.	LI	
Aquis Statiellis .	.	.	.	XXVIII	
Crixia .	.	.	.	XX	
Canalico .	.	.	.	X	
Vadis Sabatis .	.	.	.	XII	
Pullopice .	.	.	.	XII	
Albingauno .	.	.	.	XVIII (Ed. VIII.: MS. XVIIII).
Luco Bormani .	.	.	.	XV	
Costa Balenæ .	.	.	.	XVI	
Albintemelio .	.	.	.	XVI	
Lumone .	.	.	.	X	
Alpis Summa .	.	.	.	VI	
Cemenelio .	.	.	.	VIIII	
Ad Varum .	.	.	.	VI	

DCXXI

We may thus conclude that the distance from Genoa to the Var was $62 + 78 = 140$ M. P., and therefore the distance from Rome to Genoa $495 - 140 = 355$ M. P.

Of this distance, 284 M. P. lay between Rome and the Magra, and consequently 71 M. P. between the Magra and Genoa. The Magra would have been crossed at a station called in the Ant. Itin., probably in a corrupt form, *Boaceas*, lying at the confluence of the Magra and the Vara (the ancient *Boactes*). This station would be made by Pliny to be 284 M. P. from Rome.

The first station from Boaceas, on the way to Rome, was Luna, whence there were two roads to Pisæ; a direct one along the coast by Fossæ Papyrianæ, which was the regular Aurelian Way; and a longer one by Luca. It is this second one that Pliny would follow, for he mentions Luca, and not the Fossæ, as on his line of way. The route from Rome to Boaceas, by way of Luca, is thus derived from the Ant. Itin.:

Roma	M. P.
Lorio . . .	XII
Ad Turres . .	X
Pyrgos . .	XII
Castro Novo .	VIII
Centum Cellis .	V
Ad Martham .	X
Forum Aurelii .	XIIII
Cosa . . .	XXV
Ad Lacum Aprilem	XLII (Ed. XXII: st. 35).[1]

[1] If we assume the distance from Cossa to the Lacus Aprilis (*Castiglione della Pescaja*) to be 42 M. P., then the distance from Cossa to Populonium would be, according to the Itinerary, $42 + 12 + 9 + 12 = 75$ M. P. $= 600$ stadia. But Strabo says that the distance from Cossa to

		M. P.
Salebrone	. .	XII
Manliana	. .	VIIII
Populonio	. .	XII
Vadis Volaterranis		XXV
Ad Herculem	.	XVIII
Pisæ	. . .	XII
Luca	. . .	XII
Luna	. . .	XXXIII
Boaceas	. .	XII

CCLXXXIII

This is only one mile less than Pliny's 284 M. P. from the Magra to the Tiber, so that the two estimates will greatly help to confirm one another. I now turn to Strabo, who measures from Luna to the Tiber. According to Pliny, this distance would be $284 - 12 = 272$ M. P. $= 2176$ stadia. But Strabo gives this distance (p. 222) at 2500 stadia, which is also in accordance with his subsequent details:

Luna		STADIA
Pisæ	. more than	400
Volaterræ (Vada)	.	280
Populonium	. .	270
Cossa	. . .	800 ("or 600")
Graviscæ	. . .	300
Pyrgi	. not quite	180
Ostia	. . .	260

2490

Strabo's distances between Cossa and Ostia agree very nearly with the Ant. Itin., and would be sufficiently accurate; but between Luna and Cossa they are greatly exaggerated, and make the whole distance

Populonium was about 800 stadia, or, according to some, about 600: so that we may fairly infer that the distance was not less than the latter estimate.

between those places 1750 stadia. But here he has very fortunately given us himself the means of correcting him; for Polybius, he tells us, made the distance from Luna to Cossa to be 1330 stadia, instead of 1750. Now 1330 stadia make $166\frac{1}{4}$ M. P., which accords with the distance from Cossa to Luna, by Fossæ Papyrianæ or Papiriana, in the Ant. Itin.:

	M. P.	
Cosa		
Ad Lacum Aprilem	XLII	
Salebrone . .	XII	
Manliana . .	VIIII	
Populonio . .	XII	
Vadis Volaterranis	XXV	
Ad Herculem .	XVIII	
Pisæ . . .	XII	
Papiriana . .	XII	(Ed. XI: seven MSS. XII: Peut. Tab. XV).
Luna . . .	XXIIII	
	CLXVI = 1328 stadia	
Add—Boaceas .	XII	
And—Rome to Cossa	XCVI	
Rome to the Magra	CCLXXIIII	

This was the distance from Rome to Boaceas by the regular Aurelian Way, and is the estimate which I shall follow.

Our next stage is the distance from Boaceas to Genoa, which we have already found, from Pliny and other authorities, to be $211 - 140 = 71$ M. P. This distance may also be derived from the Ant. Itin., adopting the usual identifications for the stations between Boaceas and Genoa:

	M. P.	
Boaceas		
Bodetia (*Bonassola*) .	XXI	(St. 16: ed. XXVII: six MSS. XXI).

Tegulata (*Tregoso*) .   XII (St. 10).

Delphinis (*Porto Fino*)   XXI (Modern dist. 22 or 23 M. P.)

Genua .   .   .   XVII (St. 17 : ed. XII : MS. XXII : Marit. Itin. XVIII).

LXXI[1]

The Aurelian Way now takes us over the Apennines to Tortona.

Here the editions of the Ant. Itin. give XXXVI M. P. between Genoa and Libarna, and XXXV M. P. between Libarna and Tortona; thus making a total of 71 M. P. between Genoa and Tortona. But, instead of XXXVI and XXXV, the various readings, XXVI and XXV, ought to be taken, so as to make a total of 51 M. P.

This appears from four reasons:

1. The straight distance between Genoa and Tortona is 35 M. P., which the passage of the Apennines might raise to 51, but hardly to 71 M. P.

2. The modern distance from Genoa to Tortona by the most direct road is 77.08 kilomètres = 52 M. P.

3. Strabo says (p. 217) that Tortona lay midway between Placentia and Genoa. But Placentia was 51 M. P. from Tortona (*ante*, p. 70, note).

---

[1] In the Peutingerian Table the names of the stations between the Magra and Genoa are different from these, and some of the distances corrupt. I should correct the Table thus:

		M. P.
Boron (*Boaceas*) .	.	
In Alpe Pennino .	.	XV (Ed. II.: st. 12).
Monilia (*Moneglia*)	.	XIII (St. 11).
Solaria (*Zoagli*) .	.	XVI (Ed. VI.: st. 14).
Ricina (*Recco*) .	.	XV
Genua (*Genoa*) .	.	XII (Ed. VII.: st. 12).

LXXI

The station, *In Alpe Pennino* (read *In Apennino*) would be on the summit of the ridge east of Levanto and Bonassqla (*Bodetia*). Just to the west of Nervi there is a village called *Quinto*, 7 M. P. from Recco (*Ricina*), which would thus be 12 M. P. from Genoa.

4. He also says, in the same place, that Placentia and Genoa were each 400 stadia from Tortona. Now 400 stadia $=50$ M. P.

The distance from Rome to Tortona by the Aurelian Way was therefore as follows:

	M. P.
Rome	
Boaceas . . .	274
Genoa	71
Tortona . . .	51
	396

All the roads from Tortona and the east to the Cottian Alps are made to meet at Turin, which was 40 M. P. from Susa. But the ancient distance between Tortona and Turin is less easily determined. If we complete our itinerary by the modern road between those two cities, we shall get the following result:

	M. P.	
Rome		
Tortona . . .	396	
Alessandria . .	15	(9 Piedmontese miles)
Asti . . .	$24\frac{1}{2}$	($14\frac{3}{4}$ Pied. miles)
Turin . . .	$37\frac{1}{2}$	($22\frac{1}{2}$ Pied. miles)
Susa . . .	40	
	513	

This brings us within 6 M. P. of the 519 between Rome and Scingomagus. But no ancient road seems to have been as short as the modern one. In the Ant. Itin. we find no road marked from Tortona to Turin; but the Peut. Tab. gives us two. One, of which I shall say nothing, leads thither by way of Acqui, Alba, and Polenzo (*Pollentia*): the other by way of Valenza (*Forum Fulvii*), Asti, and Polenzo. The distance between Tortona and Valenza is not given; but it may be taken at 17 M. P., one mile more than

the straight distance. From Valenza to Asti, XXII
M. P. are given; which should probably be altered
into XXX or XXXII, as the straight distance is XXV
M. P., and the country between Valenza and Asti is
occupied by hills. I shall suppose the distance to be
XXX M. P. From Asti to Polenzo XVI M. P. are given:
the straight distance is 23, and the true reading therefore probably XXVI. From Polenzo to Turin XXXV
M. P. are given, which is right.

This would make the distance from Rome to Scingomagus too great for Susa, and still worse for the
other supposed sites of Scingomagus, which are about
25 or 30 M. P. further from Turin. The Peutingerian
road takes a great and unnecessary circuit by way of
Polenzo, making the distance between Asti and Turin
61 M. P., while the modern distance is only 37½. If
we replace this circuitous road by the modern one,
our itinerary to Susa would run thus:

				M. P.
Rome				
Tortona	.	.	.	396
Valenza	.	.	.	17
Asti	.	.	.	30
Turin	.	.	.	37½
Susa	.	.	.	40
				520½

This is almost accurately 519 M. P. But I doubt
whether it is the way to be followed, except as far as
Valenza on the Po. What Strabo says of the route
from Placentia to the Cottian Land is here of importance. On that route, he tells us, was Ticinum
(*Pavia*), and the river of the same name flowing into
the Po; and Clastidium, and Dertona (*Tortona*), and
Aquæ Statiellæ, a little on one side, the direct road
to Ocelum running along the rivers Po and Dora.

On this direct road (from Pavia), which is given in
the Ant. Itin., was a station called Carbantia, 50 M. P.
from Turin, and 12 from Cozzo (*Cottiæ*). Carbantia
was therefore very near Casale, which is, by the
modern road, 49½ M. P. from Turin, and 11 from
Cozzo; while no more than 14 M. P. of plain intervene
between it and Valenza. The true route to Scingomagus from Tortona would, I think, strike into this
'direct way' at Carbantia, and so proceed to Turin
and Ocelum, and on to Scingomagus.

On this supposition our itinerary would be nearly
as follows:

	M. P.
Roma	
Dertona . .	CCCXCVI
Forum Fulvii .	XVII (St. 16)
Carbantia (*Casale*)	XV (St. 14)
Rigomagus .	XII
Quadratæ . .	XV
Taurini . .	XXIII
Ad Fines . .	XVI
Segusio . .	XXIIII
	DXVIII

or only one mile short of 519 M. P. In any case, the
condition which requires that Scingomagus should be
519 M. P. from Rome is very closely satisfied by Susa.

The other three conditions will give much less
trouble.

2. Susa ought to be 71 M. P. from Embrun,
reckoned over the Mont Genèvre. The distance
between Embrun and Susa is: by the Ant. Itin. 70
M. P., by the Peut. Tab. 72 M. P., and by the modern
road 66 kilomètres + 22 Italian miles = 72 M. P.

3. Susa ought to lie at the foot of the Alps (ὑπὸ
ταῖς ᾿Αλπεσιν). Ocelum lay where the Alps began

(Strabo), that is to say, on the edge of the Italian plain: and Scingomagus, 28 M. P. within the Alps, counting from Ocelum, is yet defined, in Artemidorus' route across the Cottian Alps, as lying ὑπὸ ταῖς Ἄλπεσιν. The probable meaning would be, that Scingomagus lay where the main valley was left, and at the foot of the mountain crossed by the route :[1] so that Susa, lying at the foot of the Mont Cenis, satisfies the condition required by the words, ὑπὸ ταῖς Ἄλπεσιν ; while the Mont Cenis is probably pointed out, when Scingomagus is identified with Susa, as the mountain crossed by the route of Artemidorus. We could hardly speak of Susa as lying at the foot of the Mont Genèvre.

4. Italy ought to begin at Susa. The Jerusalem Itinerary says of Susa, *Inde incipit Italia*, just as Strabo says of Scingomagus, Ἡ ἀπὸ Σκιγγομάγου ἤδη Ἰταλία λέγεται.

Such is the evidence which fixes Scingomagus at Susa (*Segusio*), and Ocelum a little below Avigliana (*Ad Fines*). But these are not the sites most generally adopted, for the majority of geographers seem to have been guided here by mere resemblances of names, and to have disregarded more important considerations. As there are several names like Ocelum (= Welsh *uchel*, 'high') in this neighbourhood, *Esseillon* (cf. *Uxellodunum*, now the Puech d' *Issolu*), *Usseglio*, *Exilles*, and *Usseaux*, opinions have been various. D' Anville has adopted *Usseaux*, in the Val Clusone, and Cluverius *Exilles*, a few miles above Susa. For Scingomagus, D' Anville selects a hamlet called Chamlat de *Siguin*

---

[1] Tennulius, the old commentator in Hudson, is here right: "Roma ducit nos Scingomagum vicum ad initium nempe conscendendarum Alpium. Hodie *Susa* vocatur."

on the Sestrières mountain, and Cluverius, Cesanne at
the foot of the Mont Genèvre. Cesanne (*Gesdao*) was
45 M. P. from Embrun, and Usseaux is 30.87 kilomètres, rather less than 21 M. P., from Cesanne, Chamlat
de Siguin lying between the two, about 4 M. P. from
Cesanne. Exilles is about 16 M. P. below Cesanne.

The following table will thus shew how Cluverius
and D'Anville disagree with Strabo, the distances
being Roman miles:

Embrun	Strabo	Cluverius	D'Anville
Scingomagus	. 71	. 45	. 49
Ocelum .	. 28	. 16	. 17
	99	. 61	. 66

The Scingomagus of Cluverius has the advantage
over that of D'Anville in lying ὑπὸ ταῖς ʼΑλπεσιν, *i. e.*
at the foot of the Mont Genèvre; a condition over-
looked in Sillig's Pliny, where Scingomagus is placed
on the summit of the Genèvre. But both Cesanne and
Chamlat de Siguin would be rather too far from Rome;
and Ocelum, being the Roman frontier town, could not
have lain at Exilles, *above* Susa, which was the chief
town of the Cottian Land. Against D'Anville's opinion that Ocelum was at Usseaux, may be urged in
addition: that the hypothesis of an ancient road crossing the Sestrières rests upon no evidence whatever;
that the way to Usseaux can never have run παρὰ
τὸν Δουρίαν ποταμόν; and that if Usseaux were a
Roman town on the frontier of the Cottian Land, that
territory would be too much contracted, as its eastern
boundary would probably in such a case have been
formed by the dotted line in my map. We have also
no proof that Italy began, either at Cesanne or
Chamlat de Siguin. In short, of the four conditions

for the determination of the position of Ocelum, D'Anville's site would not agree with 1, 2, 3, and 4; and Cluverius' not with 2, 3, and 4 : while in the case of Scingomagus, D'Anville's site would not be in accordance with conditions 1, 2, 3, and 4; nor Cluverius' with 1, 2, and 4. Urtiola and Susa, on the contrary, satisfy all the four conditions in each case, and are fairly entitled to be considered as the sites of the ancient Ocelum and Scingomagus.

As some compensation for abandoning D'Anville when clearly right as to the position of the Medulli, Mr. Law follows him when as surely wrong with respect to the sites of Ocelum and Scingomagus, and thus precludes the Mont Cenis from being Artemidorus' pass from Scingomagus, or Cæsar's from Ocelum, over the Cottian Alps, as he formerly betrayed a similar wish to transfer the Medullian pass to the Little St. Bernard. Yet it is gratifying to find that I must have proved to his satisfaction, in our former controversy, that there was a Medullian pass, and that he no longer holds the ἀνάβασις of a mountain to be the same as its κάθετος, or perpendicular height.

CHAPTER V.

ON THE PASS OF ARTEMIDORUS (ABOUT B.C. 100) BETWEEN SCINGOMAGUS
AND TRANSALPINE GAUL—ITS PROBABLE IDENTITY WITH THAT OF
HANNIBAL—IDENTITY OF BOTH PASSES WITH THE MONT CENIS, AND
NOT THE MONT GENEVRE.

I NOW take up the enquiry where I left it at the end
of the first chapter. It was there shewn that Hannibal traversed a pass leading through the country of
the Taurini, and not the country of the Salassi. Both
the Great and Little St. Bernard are thus excluded
from any claim to be considered as Hannibal's pass,
and it only remains to determine whether he crossed
the Mont Cenis or the Mont Genèvre.

Leaving here for the present the question of Han-
nibal's pass, I turn to consider the great route between
Italy and Gaul about a century later, the pass of
Artemidorus across the Cottian Alps.

The length of the world, as known by the ancients,
was estimated by Artemidorus, who flourished about
103 B.C. (Clinton), at 71560 stadia, or 8945 M. P.
This measurement was derived from an itinerary of
several stages; one stage being from Scingomagus
(Susa) to Illiberis (Elne), or from the foot of the Alps
in Italy to the foot of the Pyrenees in Gaul. Such
a road from Scingomagus to Illiberis, the length of
which measured the extent of Gaul traversed by the
route of Artemidorus, must of necessity have crossed

G

the Cottian Alps by some pass.   The question which
arises is: Was this pass the pass of the Mont Cenis or
the Mont Genèvre? The distance between Scingomagus and Illiberis must decide the question.

Now the route of Artemidorus is preserved by two
authors; Agathemerus (Hudson, *Geogr. Græc. Minor.*
vol. ii.), and Pliny. In the first the distances are given
in stadia, in the second in Roman miles of 8 stadia
each.   Let us first consider the distance between
Scingomagus and Illiberis, as it is to be deduced from
Agathemerus.

It happens that there is a *lacuna* in Agathemerus
where this distance should be found; and it must
therefore be calculated by subtracting from the total
distance from the Ganges to Gades (71560 stadia) the
sum of all the component distances with the exception
of the missing distance in question.   In one of these
component distances there is, however, a gross error
which must be previously corrected.

The distance from Illiberis to the coast opposite
Gades, a distance which measures the length of Spain
traversed by the route, is given in Agathemerus at
2651 stadia $= 331\frac{3}{8}$ M. P.   This agrees with the editions
of Pliny, where the distance is given at 332 M. P.,
though one of the best MSS. (A in Sillig) gives 832,
reading DCCCXXXII instead of CCCXXXII.

It is evident that 832, and not 332 M. P., is the
distance to be taken, as the straight distance is more
than 700 M. P. The same appears also from Pliny
(III. 3, 4) and Strabo; the last of whom, in his
description of the country between Gades and the
Pyrenees, continually refers to Artemidorus, and never
intimates any disagreement with him in the matter of
distances.   Pliny gives:

	M. P.
Gades	
Castulo	250
Pyrenees	607
	857
Deduct passage of strait to Gades	7½
	849½
Add from Pyrenees to Illiberis	17
	866½

Strabo gives:

	STADIA
Gades	
Calpe	750 (pp. 140, 168)
Carthago Nova. . .	2200 (p. 156)
Ebro	2200 (σχεδόν τι, p. 156)
Pompey's trophies . .	1600 (p. 156)
	6750
Deduct passage of strait to Gades	60
	6690
Add from Pompey's trophies to Illiberis	136
	6826 = 853¼ M. P.

This is the distance by the *coast* road, which, according to Pliny (III. 3, 4), was rather more than 25 M. P. in excess of the distance by the road through Castulo. Deduct these 25 M. P. from 853¼, and there remain 828¼.

These considerations are enough to shew that DCCCXXXII, not CCCXXXII, is the true reading in Pliny, and that Agathemerus would have written ͵ϛχνα' (6651), not ͵βχνα' (2651) stadia. For 6651 stadia make 831⅜ M. P.

Adopting this correction, the route of Artemidorus, as given by Agathemerus, would run thus:

Ganges		STADIA
Euphrates	. .	41350[1]
Mazaca	. . .	2550[2]
Ephesus	. . .	3320

Total from Ganges to Ephesus　47220

Total also by addition	. .	47220
Delos	. . .	1600
Isthmus	. . .	1700
Patræ	. . .	720
Leucas	. . .	700
Corcyra	. . .	700
Acroceraunia	. .	600
Brundusium	. .	700
Rome	. . .	2880
Scingomagus	. .	4152
Illiberis	. . .	(caret)
Port of Gades	. .	6651
Gades	. . .	60

Total	. . .	71560
Total by addition	.	67743 (+ the distance from Scingomagus to Illiberis)
Difference	. .	3817 stadia = 477⅛ M. P.

[1] In a previous itinerary the details are thus given:

Indus	. . . .	16000
Caspian Gates	. .	15300
Euphrates	. . .	10050
		41350

Strabo, following Eratosthenes, with whom Artemidorus (p. 663) agrees, gives the distances thus:

Indus	. . .	16000 (p. 64)
Caspian Gates	.	15300 (p. 723)
Euphrates	. .	10000 (pp. 64, 79)
		41300

[2] As will be afterwards noticed more particularly, this distance and the following are incorrect, though their sum is very nearly right.

This difference would be the distance from Scingomagus to Illiberis, which thus appears from Agathemerus to have been, omitting the fraction, 477 M. P.

I now proceed to examine the route as given by
Pliny.

Three of the distances in Pliny would be incorrect.
Two of them are: the total, and the distance from
Corcyra to Acroceraunia. Here the statements of
Pliny and Agathemerus are, in M. P.:

	PLINY.	AGATHEMERUS.
Total . . .	LXXXIX.XCV[1]	LXXXIX.XLV.
Corcyra to Acroceraunia	CXXXIID	LXXXIID.

That we ought to read, in the last case, LXXXIID for
CXXXIID, is plain from three considerations:

1. The straight distance is not more than 70 M. P.

2. Strabo (p. 105) makes the distance 700 stadia,
= 87½ M. P.

3. Strabo (p. 324) says that the length of the
voyage from Acroceraunia to the entrance of the
Ambracian Gulf, i. e. to within a few miles of Leucas,
was 1300 stadia = 162½ M. P. But Pliny and Agathemerus both make the distance from Leucas to
Corcyra to be 87½ M. P. Therefore the distance from
Corcyra to Acroceraunia slightly exceeded 162½ − 87½
= 75 M. P.: i. e. it was 82½, not 132½ M. P.

Pliny's total would probably have been increased
50 M. P. by the error in the stage from Corcyra to
Acroceraunia, and ought thus to be altered, so as
to agree with Agathemerus, from LXXXIX.XCV to
LXXXIX.XLV.

The third error in Pliny's distances would be in

---

[1] The MS. readings are: LXXXIX.XC———LXXXIX.XCV———LXXXLX.XCII
———LXXXIV.II.

the distance from the Isthmus of Corinth to Patræ. This is given as CCIID M. P., which ought to be XCIID M. P.   For:—

1. The straight distance does not exceed 70 M. P.

2. Pliny (IV. 5) makes the distance from Patræ to the head of the Corinthian Gulf to be 85 M. P.; the width of the Isthmus to be 5 M. P.; and (incorrectly) the distance of Corinth from *either* shore to be 60 stadia = $7\frac{1}{2}$ M. P.

3. Agathemerus makes the distance from the Isthmus to Patræ 720 stadia = 90 M. P.

All Pliny's other distances would be correct; and his itinerary, omitting the distance from Scingomagus to Illiberis, would be as follows:

					M. P.
Ganges					
Euphrates	.	.	.	.	5169
Mazaca	.	.	.	.	244[1]
Ephesus	.	.	.	.	498[2]

---

[1] Here Pliny and Agathemerus greatly differ, as Pliny gives 244 M. P., while Agathemerus gives 2550 stadia = $318\frac{3}{4}$ M. P.   Pliny is right.   The station on the Euphrates was apparently (Strabo, p. 663) Tomisa, not far from Melitene.   But the straight distance from Mazaca to Tomisa is very accurately 200 M. P.; and the Antonine Itinerary (ed. Parthey and Pinder) gives 228 M. P. as the distance between Mazaca and Melitene.

[2] There is another great discrepancy here between Pliny and Agathemerus.   While Pliny gives 498 M. P., Agathemerus gives 3320 stadia = 415 M. P. between Mazaca and Ephesus.   Pliny is again right.   Strabo (p. 663) traces this route completely through seventeen intermediate stations.   The sum of his distances is 3800 stadia and a little more, or 475 M. P. and a little more.   From Carura to Holmi (site unknown) he allows 920 stadia, and from Holmi to Tyriæum 500 stadia and a little more; thus giving 1420 stadia and a little more, = $177\frac{1}{2}$ M. P. and a little more, between Carura and Tyriæum.   But the straight distance from Carura to Tyriæum is 195 M. P., which would give a travelling distance of fully 200 M. P.   Strabo's 'little more' (if his distances are correct) would thus amount to 23 M. P.; so that his 475 M. P. and a little more would agree with Pliny's 498 M. P.

It will be observed that there is only a difference, neglecting fractions,

				M. P.
Delos .	.	.	.	200
Isthmus	.	.	.	212½
Patræ	.	.	.	92½
Leucas	.	.	.	87½
Corcyra	.	.	.	87½
Acroceraunia	.	.		82½
Brundusium	.	.		87½
Rome	.	.	.	360[1]
Scingomagus	.	.		519
Illiberis	.	.	.	
Coast opposite Gades	.			832
Gades	.	.	.	7½

Total	.	.	.	8945
Total by addition .		.	.	8479½ (+ the distance from Scingomagus to Illiberis)

Difference .		.	465½

This would be the distance from Scingomagus to Illiberis. And this is confirmed by the MS. readings of Pliny for this distance, which are :

CCCLI

CCCLVI

CCCCLIII

CCCCCLVI

CCCCCLXVI

which shew that the distance was probably 466 M. P., though 456 M. P. would be more probable. On the whole, as neither CCC nor CCCCC can be admitted for

of 8 M. P. between Pliny and Agathemerus in the whole distance of about 740 M. P. from the Euphrates to Ephesus : indeed, the distances of Agathemerus would be very accurate, if the intermediate station between the Euphrates and Ephesus were not Mazaca, but the frontier town of Cappadocia, Garsaura, which Strabo makes 680 stadia, or 85 M. P. from Mazaca. The itinerary commonly reckons from frontier places.

[1] So also Strabo (p. 283), as well as Agathemerus.

the number of hundreds, we may safely infer, from Pliny and Agathemerus, that the distance from Scingomagus (Susa) to Illiberis (Elne), by the Pass of Artemidorus, was most probably 466 m. p., and lay at any rate between 451 and 477 m. p.

We have another authority for this conclusion.

According to Strabo (p. 105), Polybius made the distance from Narbonne to the Straits of Messina (probably Rhegium) to be more than 11200 stadia, or 1400 m. p. To see how this distance was made up, it will first be necessary to determine the distance between Rome and Rhegium.

Now the total distance from Rome to 'the Column' is given in the Ant. Itin. at 455 m. p., or, according to one ms., 460. From 'the Column' to Rhegium, Strabo and Pliny give 100 stadia or $12\frac{1}{2}$ m. p., the Peut. Tab. 6 m. p., and the inscription of Polla 5 m. p. This makes the distance from Rome to Rhegium to lie between 460 and $472\frac{1}{2}$ m. p.

Strabo, in accordance with Pliny and Agathemerus, gives (p. 283) the distance from Rome to Brundusium at 360 m. p., and adds that the distance from Rome to Rhegium was three or four days' journey more; which increase of length is the same as the width that he allows for the isthmus of Suez (p. 35), and which he states elsewhere (p. 803) to be 900 stadia, though his epitomater and Agrippa (Pliny v. 12) allow 1000, the straight distance, however, being only 600. Now 360 m. p. + 900 stadia = $472\frac{1}{2}$ m. p.

Pliny (iii. 6) makes the distance from Augusta Prætoria to Rhegium, by a circuitous road through Rome and Capua, to be 1020 m. p. Now the distance from Augusta Prætoria to Rome is found by the following calculation:

Augusta Prætoria				M. P.	
Eporedia	.	.	.	46	⎫
Vercellæ	.	.	.	33	⎬ (Ant. Itin.)
Laumellum		.	.	25	⎪
Ticinum	.	.	.	22	⎭
Placentia	.	.	.	36	(Strabo, p. 217)
Rome	.	.	.	392	(*ante*, p. 70, note)

$$\overline{}$$

554

which leaves, for the distance from Rome to Rhegium, $1020 - 554 = 466$ M. P.

This, which lies between the two extremes of 460 and $472\frac{1}{2}$ M. P., was probably the true distance.

From Rome to Scingomagus both Pliny and Agathemerus give 519 M. P. as the distance. Therefore (if the whole distance from the Straits of Messina to Narbonne is reckoned, as appears to be the case, over the Cottian Alps)[1] the distance from Scingomagus to Narbonne would exceed $1400 - 466 - 519 = 415$ M. P. Add the distance between Narbonne and Illiberis, which was 47 M. P., and the whole distance between Scingomagus and Illiberis would be more than 462 M. P., which agrees with Pliny's 466, and Agathemerus' 477.

It may not be out of place here to shew how Polybius probably made out the distance between the Straits of Messina and Narbonne to be more than 11200 stadia.

It is by lengths of 200 stadia that he reckons

---

[1] It is certainly not reckoned, as might be expected, over the Maritime Alps. For Strabo's longest estimate (p. 178) of the distance from the Pyrenees to the Var is 2800 stadia, or 350 M. P.; which gives, from Narbonne to the Var, $350 - 63$ (*ib.*) $= 287$ M. P. Add, with Pliny, 495 from the Var to the Tiber (or Rome); and allow 466 from Rome to Rhegium. The result is only $466 + 495 + 287 = 1248$ M.P., which is above 150 M. P. too little.

distances. Now, as we are told by Strabo (p. 105), Polybius made Narbonne to be less than 8000 stadia from the Pillars of Hercules. But Polybius, in his account of Hannibal's march to the Alps, makes the distance from the Pillars to the Rhone to be 8800 stadia. Therefore the distance from Narbonne to the Rhone was more than 800 stadia. From the passage of the Rhone to the commencement of the Alps, Polybius gives in the same place 1400 stadia, and estimates the length of the route across the Alps at 1200 stadia. This last stage would terminate at Avigliana, 24 miles below Scingomagus (Susa), and consequently $519 - 24 = 495$ M. P. from Rome. This distance Polybius would reckon at 4000 stadia $=$ 500 M. P., as he probably would the distance from Rome to Rhegium, 466 M. P., at 3800 stadia $= 475$ M. P. His whole distance from the Straits of Messina to Narbonne would thus amount to what he gives in Strabo, more than 11200 stadia. For it would be made up in the following manner:

	STADIA
Rhegium	
Rome	3800
Foot of Alps . . .	4000
End of Alpine route . .	1200
Passage of Rhone . .	1400
Narbonne . more than	800
Total more than	11200

Let us now return to consider the Pass of Artemidorus, which thus appears, as would have been anticipated, to have been identical with 'the pass through the country of the Taurini, which Hannibal crossed,' the most ancient road across the Cottian Alps. This road was not identical with the ordinary road across the Genèvre. For the route across the Genèvre is given both by Strabo and the Roman Itineraries; and the correctness of their statements is satisfactorily established by the known position of most of the stations, and the modern distances between them. In Strabo's route the Rhone is crossed at Tarascon; in that of the Itineraries at Arles. The following are the distances in Roman miles by the two routes:

STRABO.			ITINERARIES.		
Scingomagus	M. P.		Segusio	M. P.	
Ebrodunum	.	71 (99 − 28, p. 179)	Ebrodunum	70	
Tarasco .	.	162 (99 + 63, *ibid.*)	Arelate	.	169
Nemausus	.	15[1]	Nemausus	19	
Narbo .	.	90 (720 stadia, p. 187)[2]	Narbo	.	91
Ruscino	.	40 (Ant. Itin.)	Ruscino	.	40
Illiberis .	.	7 (Peut. Tab.)[3]	Illiberis	.	7
		———			———
		385			396

Neither of these could be the route of Artemidorus, which was probably 466 M. P. in length. In fact, none of the estimates derived from Pliny for the distance between Scingomagus and Illiberis will suit the route over the Genèvre; not even the most favourable, which would be CCCLXVI M. P. Nor could this reading be admitted; for it could not be reconciled with the rest of the itinerary from India to Gades.

The length of the route from Susa to Elne by the Mont Cenis agrees with the distance between those two places as given by Artemidorus. I have, in my Treatise on Hannibal's passage of the Alps, calculated the distance from Susa to Valence by the Little Mont

---

[1] So in Peut. Tab.: straight, 15: trabo (p. 187), about 100 stadia = 12½ M. P.

[2] 88 M. P., p. 178.

[3] The straight distance from Narbonne to Elne is 45 M. P.

Cenis at 196 M. P.[1]   Assuming this to be correct, the whole distance to Illiberis would be as follows :

Segusio	M. P.	
Valentia	.	196
Arelate .	.	114 (Jerus. Itin.: modern dist.; by road, 111; by railway, 109).
Nemausus	.	19 (Straight, 18).
Narbo .	.	91 (Straight, 88).
Ruscino .	.	40
Illiberis	.	7
		——
		467

If the Rhone were crossed at Tarascon, the distance would be about 10 or 12 M. P. less.

From this it would appear that the Mont Cenis was the Cottian Pass of Hannibal, Polybius, and Artemidorus; and that the route of the Mont Genèvre (at least as traced by Strabo and in the Antonine Itinerary) was yet unopened up to the year 100 B.C., although the Mont Genèvre is a lower and easier pass than the Mont Cenis, and about 70 M. P. would be saved by taking it.

There is, however, an ancient route by the Genèvre, which would agree very well in point of distance with that of Polybius and Artemidorus.   This route is the one given in the Jerusalem Itinerary.   It coincides with the route of the Antonine Itinerary as far as Gap, and then ceases to follow the Durance to Sisteron, and so to proceed to Apt, and Arles or Tarascon, but strikes off towards the north-west over the Col de Câbre (*Mons Gaura*) to Die and Valence, where it

---

[1] By the high road over the *Great* Mont Cenis, Montmélian on the Isère is 61 Piedmontese miles = 102 M. P. from Susa; and Montmélian is 147 kilomètres, or 99 M. P. from Valence. This gives 201 M. P. between Susa and Valence.

falls into the road from the Mont Cenis to Avignon, Tarascon, and Arles.

By this route over the Genèvre the distances are as follow:

Segusio		M. P.	
Vapincum	.	99	
Lucus	. .	50	(Ant. Itin.: Jerus. Itin. 56; modern road, 46).
Valentia	.	57	(Ant. Itin.: Jerus. Itin. 62; modern road, 59).
Arelate	. .	114	
Nemausus	.	19	
Narbo	. .	91	
Ruscino	.	40	
Illiberis	. .	7	
		477	

or, crossing the Rhone at Tarascon, about 10 or 12 miles less.

But there are difficulties in supposing this route to be that of Hannibal, Polybius, and Artemidorus. It could not, for several reasons, have been that of Hannibal, one of which seems conclusive. Hannibal proceeded from the confluence of the Rhone and Isère for about 800 stadia, or 100 M. P., παρὰ τὸν ποταμόν, before he began to ascend the Alps; while the *summit* of the Mons Gaura lies no more than about 70 M. P. from that confluence. The next chapter, however, will dissipate any claims which the last road may have left to be considered as the ancient road through the Cottian Alps.[1]

---

[1] Artemidorus' road from Ephesus to Mazaca, which Strabo calls " a highway trodden by all going from Ephesus to the East," is not found in the Antonine Itinerary. A similar omission has been considered almost a conclusive argument against the existence of an ancient route over the Mont Cenis.

CHAPTER VI.

IT may have caused some surprise that the route of
the Mont Cenis should appear, from the distances
given by Polybius and Artemidorus, to have been
the great line of communication between Spain and
Cisalpine Gaul, and to have been taken as such by
Hannibal, while the lower and easier pass of the
Genèvre would have shortened the journey by about
70 M. P.   But the subject which we are now going to
consider will explain this.   The pass of the Mont
Genèvre was not opened till the year 76 B.C.

When Pompey marched in that year against Ser-
torius in Spain, he wrote a letter to the Senate, which
is preserved in the fragments of Sallust.   Pompey's
words are :

> Diebus quadraginta exercitum paravi, hostesque in cervici-
> bus jam Italiæ agentes ab Alpibus in Hispaniam summovi :
> *per eas iter aliud atque Hannibal, nobis opportunius, patefeci.*

From this I shall draw several conclusions :

1. The route noticed at the end of the last Chapter, by the Mont Genèvre and the Mons Gaura to
Valence, was not the ancient route across the Alps

from the country of the Taurini into Gaul: for in
that case the new pass which Pompey opened would
be only the route from Gap down the Durance to
Tarascon and Arles.

2. The Mont Cenis was an ancient pass. It will,
I think, be granted, that Hannibal did not cross the
Great St. Bernard. Let us suppose then, for the sake
of argument, that he crossed the Little St. Bernard.
In this case Polybius would give us two passes south
of the Little St. Bernard; namely, his Ligurian pass
and his pass through the Taurini. Pompey's route,
being a more convenient route between Italy and
Spain than that of Hannibal, would also lie south of
the Little St. Bernard. In that part of the Alps
there were then three ancient passes, which we may
fairly identify with the pass of Turbia or Corniche
road, the Mont Genèvre, and the Mont Cenis.

3. Hannibal crossed the Mont Cenis. I believe
I have proved in my first chapter that he crossed
a pass leading through the country of the Taurini,
and not through that of the Salassi. Hannibal, that
is to say, crossed the Cottian Alps, as also Pompey
must have done, for the Ligurian pass was open
before his time. Of the two passes then, the Mont
Cenis and the Mont Genèvre, one was crossed by
Hannibal, and the other by Pompey. But Pompey
crossed the more convenient pass of the two, which
is the Mont Genèvre; and therefore the Mont Cenis
was crossed by Hannibal.

The original Cottian territory, as I have already
shewn, was limited by the Mont Cenis, but included
the pass of the Mont Genèvre; extending on the
French side nearly 40 M. P., and on the Italian nearly
60 M. P., from the summit of that mountain. Bearing

this in mind, I think we may trace a not improbable connexion between the two following events:

B.C. 89. The Cottian communities become *municipia* by the Law of Pompeius Strabo.

B.C. 76. His son, Pompey the Great, opens the pass of the Mont Genèvre.

Varro's five passes between Italy and Gaul.

We have just seen that there would have been three ancient passes south of the Little St. Bernard; namely, the Mont Cenis, the Mont Genèvre, and the Pass of Turbia. The addition of the Great and Little St. Bernard would raise to the number of five the ancient passes between Italy and Gaul. And that there were five such passes we find to be the case from the authority of Varro, whose opinion must be considered of very great weight. He had written on the Second Punic War: he was one of Pompey's lieutenants in Spain when the civil war between Pompey and Cæsar broke out: and his long life extended for nearly ninety years from 116 B.C.

Varro's statement on the subject is transmitted to us by Servius in his Commentary on the Æneid (x. 13), and is twice noticed by Cluverius in his *Italia*. The passage of Servius runs thus:

Alpes quinque viis Varro dicit transiri posse: una, quæ est juxta mare, per Ligures: altera, qua Hannibal transiit: tertia, qua Pompeius ad Hispaniense bellum profectus est: quarta, qua Hasdrubal de Gallia in Italiam venit: quinta, quæ quondam a Græcis possessa est, quæ exinde Alpes Graiæ adpellantur.

If it be admitted, as I believe will be done, that Hannibal could not have crossed the Great St. Bernard, then these five passes of Varro can only be identified in the following manner:

Ligurian Pass————Pass of Turbia.
Hannibal's Pass ——Mont Cenis.
Pompey's Pass ——Mont Genèvre.
Hasdrubal's Pass ——Great St. Bernard.
Graian Pass ————Little St. Bernard.

This is the same arrangement as that made by Cluverius, with the exception that he interchanges the Mont Cenis and the Great St. Bernard; supposing that Hannibal crossed the latter of these passes, and thus saying with the respect to the Mont Cenis: "Hac igitur via *Hasdrubal* in Italiam venerît necesse est, quando nulla alia reliqua est." But it is to *Hannibal*, and not to *Hasdrubal*, that this reasoning would apply; for Hasdrubal may have crossed, as he probably did, the Great St. Bernard; while Hannibal could not have done so. Thus, only the passes of the Genèvre and Cenis remain for Hannibal and Pompey; and of these the shorter and more convenient route to Spain, namely, the Mont Genèvre, would be the one that Pompey took. No pass but that of the Cenis is consequently left for Hannibal.

I do not know how the evidence of Pompey and Varro is to be met by those who suppose that Hannibal crossed the Little St. Bernard, and who deny that the Mont Cenis was an ancient pass; although they might perhaps prefer the authority of Livy and his followers to that of Varro, and thus make the passes of Hannibal and Hasdrubal to be the same. But even this supposition, if admitted to be true, would hardly be enough to destroy the force of the words, *Alpes quinque viis Varro dicit transiri posse.* And if it did destroy their force, it would go too far: as it

H

would reduce the number of passes between Italy and Gaul, not to four, but to three; for three of Varro's passes, the pass of Hannibal, the pass of Hasdrubal, and the Graian pass, would have to be considered as one.

If the Great St. Bernard were the pass of Hasdrubal, it would also be Polybius' Salassian pass. And there is some additional evidence that the Great St. Bernard was a more ancient pass than the Little St. Bernard. For Livy (v. 34, 35) brings the Gauls who expelled the Etruscans from the plains of the Po over the Taurine and Pennine passes. It may be said indeed, and with some reason, that the Romans are not likely to have known about passages of the Alps that took place at so remote a period. This may be true: but it is quite possible that the Etruscans would have known by what passes the Gauls invaded their country; and there would probably have been Etruscan authorities for the Romans to consult, if they had chosen to do so.

There is, however, one authority in favour of a certain antiquity for the pass of the the Little St. Bernard. We learn from Livy (XXI. 38) that Cœlius Antipater, who flourished about 123 B.C. (Clinton), considered that Hannibal crossed the Alps by the *Cremonis jugum*. This pass Livy clearly considers identical with the Graian Alp, or Little St. Bernard; an opinion strengthened by the existence of a mountain called the *Crammont* in that neighbourhood. I mention this circumstance because it affords the only argument of any validity in favour of the theory that Hannibal crossed the Little St. Bernard; for the passage which Messrs. Wickham and Cramer cite from the life of Hannibal by Nepos is not to the point.

"Our opinion," they say (p. 31), "derives no small support from his (Nepos') authority, seeing that he positively asserts this to have been the Carthaginian general's route. His opinion is clear, plain, and precise. *Ad Alpes posteaquam venit, quæ Italiam ab Gallia sejungunt, quas nemo unquam cum exercitu ante, præter Herculem Graium transierat (quo facto is hodie saltus Graius appellatur), Alpicos conantes prohibere transitum concidit: loca patefecit, itinera muniit, effecitque ut ea elephantus ornatus ire posset, qua antea unus homo inermis vix poterat repere.*" It is not positively asserted here that the army of Hannibal followed the same route across the Alps that was taken by the army of Hercules the Greek; nor is perhaps the authority of Nepos, however plain and precise as to this passage of Hercules, sufficient to prove the existence of a military road over the Little St. Bernard from about 1200 B.C. Was it with the view of setting aside, in favour of Hannibal, any pretensions which Hercules, who brought the herds of Geryon over the Graian Alp, might prefer to such relics, that Messrs. W. and C. told us (p. 94) that the fossil bones of animals found near the foot of the Little St. Bernard were reported to be "much larger than those of oxen"?[1]

---

[1] The word *Cremo(n)* probably contains the Celtic roots of *Graius Mons*, which may be: *ciar*, 'canus'; *monadh*, 'mons.' It must be remembered that in the time of Cœlius there would have been no such division of the Alps as the 'Cottian.' What Alps were afterwards so called were probably then either 'Graian' or 'Maritime.'

CHAPTER VII.

DECLINE OF THE PASS OF THE MONT CENIS IN IMPORTANCE AFTER THE
OPENING OF THE MONT GENEVRE—ON CÆSAR'S PASSAGE OF THE
ALPS FROM OCELUM TO THE COUNTRY OF THE SEGUSIANI (B.C. 58)—
EFFECTED BY THE MONT CENIS—ON THE ROUTE OF PLANCUS (B.C.
43) FROM GRENOBLE TO THE RIVER VERDON.

THE connexion of the Cottian communities with the
Roman state as *municipia*, and the opening of the pass
of the Mont Genèvre by Pompey, would have greatly
impaired the importance of the pass of the Mont Cenis.
The Romans could now avail themselves of the Cottian
Land as a well-affected territory extending almost
through the Alps, between unsubdued mountaineers
on the south and north, from the plains of Cisalpine
Gaul on the east to the Vocontian country on the
west, from which the Cottian Land would only have
been separated by a tract of no very great breadth,
occupied by the Uceni, Tricorii, Caturiges, Sogiontii,
and Brigiani.

But the pass of the Mont Cenis would not have
lost its importance all at once. As a route to Spain
it would indeed have been immediately superseded by
Pompey's new route over the Genèvre, which would
have proceeded to Arles and Tarascon; but as a route
to Lyons it would probably have still been used,
though other lines of road may afterwards have caused
it to be neglected, as it certainly was, in the times of

the Empire. Two of these later lines of road branched off from Pompey's road at Gap; one proceeding by the Col de Câbre (*Mons Gaura*) to Die and Valence, and so on to Lyons; and the other by the Col de St. Guigues to Grenoble. The last of these roads was known to the Romans as early as 43 B.C.;[1] but it is not certain when the first was opened. Cæsar's passage of the Alps (B.C. 58) would have been effected by the Genèvre and one of these roads, or else by the Mont Cenis. I believe myself that he crossed the Mont Cenis. Messrs. Wickham and Cramer take him by the Mont Genèvre, Die, and Valence, though the cause of the Mont Genèvre would be better supported if the route from Gap to Grenoble were taken.

As Cæsar eventually crossed the Rhone above its confluence with the Saône, and thus entered the country of the Segusiani, we may presume, in comparing the different routes he is considered to have taken, that his march was directed upon Lyons.

The route which I suppose Cæsar to have pursued from Italy, would have coincided with that of Hannibal as far as St. Jean de Maurienne, and then have taken a direct line westward to Villard Bonnot in the valley of the Isère, by the Col de la Croix de Fer and the Col de la Coche. This would explain what Cæsar meant by saying that he took the shortest way into Transalpine Gaul. My attention was first directed to this route by the following note in Pilot's *Histoire de Grenoble*, p. 7 :

" Il y avait une autre route qui traversait les montagnes

---

[1] There is another road from Grenoble to the south, nearly parallel to this, and falling into Pompey's road at Sisteron, after crossing the pass of the Croix Haute. This might be supposed to be the ancient line of road, and I have therefore mentioned it : but I shall not refer to it again.

de Theys pour aller dans la Maurienne. On en trouve
encore une partie considerable qui se dirige vers le col de
la Coche ; elle est pavée en blocs bruts de granit, et a près
de dix pieds de largeur. On raconte communément que
César est entré dans les Gaules par ce chemin, lorsqu'il
partit d'Aquilée."

From Villard Bonnot I suppose Cæsar's route to
have proceeded to Grenoble, to have crossed the Isère
somewhere in that neighbourhood, and to have reached
Lyons by way of Bergusia or Bergusium (*Bourgoin*).

The distance from Susa to Lyons by the Little
Mont Cenis may be thus estimated. From Susa to
St. Jean de Maurienne, by the high road over the
Great Mont Cenis, the distance is given at 38 Piedmontese miles = 63 M. P. By the Little Mont Cenis,
which saves about 7 M. P., the distance would be
63 − 7 = 56 M. P. It is an ordinary day's walk over
the Col de la Croix de Fer, from St. Jean to Rivier
d' Allemont;[1] and another over the Col de la Coche to
Grenoble : so that the distance between St. Jean and
Grenoble would be about 50 M. P. Grenoble is 108
kilomètres = 73 M. P. from Lyons. From Susa to
Lyons the distance would thus be 179 M. P.

There is one circumstance in connexion with this
distance which I may touch upon before going on with
the consideration of Cæsar's route. If we add to the
179 M. P. between Susa (Scingomagus) and Lyons the
519 M. P. between Scingomagus and Rome, the whole
distance from Rome to Lyons would be 698 M. P.
Now it has been noticed by Mr. Merivale (*Hist. Rome*,
vol. I., p. 286, note) that "Cicero (pro. Quint. 25) asserts that the distance (from Rome) to the territory

---

[1] From Rivier to St. Michel, about seven English miles beyond St.
Jean, I found it a long day's journey, which I estimated at one of thirty
English miles.

of the Segusiani (Lyons) was seven hundred Roman miles." It appears from the mention of Vada Volaterrana in the oration, which was delivered before Pompey opened his route through the Alps, that the road to Lyons followed the Aurelian Way. But the accordance of distance is no decisive proof that Cicero was speaking of the route which I have supposed Cæsar to pursue. For two other ancient routes would give nearly the same distance. By the Little Mont Cenis, Chambéry, and the Mont du Chat, I calculate the distance between Rome and Lyons at 696 M. P.; and by the Little St. Bernard and the Mont du Chat (supposing an ancient road to lie through Casale from Valenza to Vercelli), at 711 M. P. But the Mont du Chat was probably not yet open; for Strabo thought (p. 208) that the Great St. Bernard afforded a shorter route than the Little St. Bernard from Aosta to Lyons. The distances are: Great St. Bernard (shortest modern road by Thonon, Geneva, and Nantua), 218 M. P.; Little St. Bernard and Mont du Chat, 188 M. P.

To return to Cæsar's route, which is thus described in his own words (*B. G.* I. 10): "Ipse (Cæsar) in Italiam magnis itineribus contendit; duasque ibi legiones conscribit; et tres, quæ circa Aquileiam hiemabant, ex hibernis educit; et, qua proximum iter in ulteriorem Galliam per Alpes erat, cum his quinque legionibus ire contendit. Ibi Centrones, et Garoceli, et Caturiges, locis superioribus occupatis, itinere exercitum prohibere conantur. Compluribus his prœliis pulsis, ab Ocelo, quod est citerioris provinciæ extremum, in fines Vocontiorum ulterioris provinciæ die septimo pervenit: inde in Allobrogum fines, ab Allobrogibus in Segusianos exercitum ducit. Hi sunt extra provinciam trans Rhodanum primi."

The first point to which I would call attention here is, that Cæsar passed from the Vocontian into the Allobrogic territory. We must therefore see where these two peoples touched one another. Now four contacts with the Allobroges have been noticed above (Chap. III.). These are : of the Segalauni and Tricastini (Ptolemy), the last of which is doubtful; of the Vocontii (Strabo); and of the Medulli (Ptolemy). The Vocontii would consequently have touched the Allobroges between the Valentinois and the Maurienne; that is to say, in the district of Grenoble. Their actual frontier towards the east cannot be assigned.

It is not necessary to suppose that Cæsar did more than touch upon the Vocontian territory, though his account might imply that he traversed it. But, literally interpreted, the following words would signify that he entered the Allobrogic territory from the Vocontian frontier which he had previously reached : " In fines Vocontiorum pervenit : *inde* in Allobrogum fines, ab Allobrogibus in Segusianos exercitum ducit."

Cæsar took the shortest way into Transalpine Gaul. The three roads between which we have to decide would separate at Susa (Scingomagus), whence the distances to Lyons would be, in M. P. :

LITTLE MONT CENIS.		GENEVRE AND GRENOBLE.		GENEVRE AND VALENCE.	
St. Jean de Maurienne	56	Gap . .	99	Gap . . .	99
Grenoble	50	Grenoble .	68 (101 kil.)	Valence . .	107
Lyons	73	Lyons .	73	Lyons . .	69
	179		240		275

The Little Mont Cenis is greatly the shortest of these three routes. It is also an additional objection to the last of them that Cæsar would not pass from the Vocontian into the Allobrogic territory. It might indeed be said that Tacitus (*Hist.* I. 66), when describing the march of Valens from Vienne to Luc, speaks of his army as "per fines Allobrogum et Vocontiorum ductus:" but this would hardly be a sufficient answer to the objection.

If Cæsar took the route of the Genèvre to Die and Valence, his Vocontian frontier would apparently be at Ad Fines, which the Jerusalem Itinerary places XI M. P. west of Gap, aud thus 39 M. P. from Embrun; though it may be doubted whether Gap did not rather belong to the Vocontii than to the Caturiges. Supposing, however, that the Vocontian frontier lay 39 M. P. from Embrun, it would be $99 + 39 = 138$ M. P. from Ocelum, which would agree exceedingly well with Cæsar's seven days' march from Ocelum to the Vocontian frontier. By the Little Mont Cenis, the distance to Grenoble, near which the Vocontian frontier lay, would be $28 + 56 + 50 = 134$ M. P., so that the two routes would in this respect be equally probable. I do not know whether Messrs. W. and C. will be considered to have made their route more or less probable by fixing Ocelum at Usseaux, and thus reducing the length of Cæsar's seven days' march thence to the Vocontian frontier from 138 to 105 M. P. Nor is it of any consequence to enquire, for Strabo's distance of 99 M. P. from Embrun to Ocelum has been already shewn to be correct (Chap. IV.), and must therefore stand.

The most conclusive evidence as to the line of Cæsar's route is derived from the names of the tribes who opposed his passage, the Centrones, the Garoceli, and the Caturiges. One of these names, the Garoceli, is new: their place is indicated by the fact that St.

Jean de Maurienne is called in old documents *Sanctus Joannes Garocellius*. Many authors, says Grillet in his *Dictionnaire du Mont Blanc et du Léman*, consider that the Maurienne was occupied by the Garoceli, "fondant leur sentiment sur plusieurs chartes de la cathédrale de Maurienne, qui donnent le nom de St. Jean des Garocelles à cette ville épiscopale" (vol. iii. p. 8). The bishopric of Maurienne was in existence as early as 341 A.D. (*ib.*). The Garoceli, whose name is to be explained from the Welsh *goruchel*, 'very high,' thus appear to be identical with the Medulli, οἵπερ τὰς ὑψηλοτάτας ἔχουσι κορυφάς, or perhaps with the southern and highest part of them above the defile of Hermillon.

Let us now see how the circumstance of Cæsar's passage being opposed by the Centrones (Tarentaise), the Garoceli, and the Caturiges, agrees with the route of the Mont Genèvre, as traced by Messrs. W. and C. In the Cottian Land Cæsar may be presumed to have met with no hostility: first, because the Cottian communities were *municipia;* and secondly, because neither the Segusini nor Quadiates, nor any of the Cottian tribes, are mentioned as offering him any opposition. At Embrun he would encounter his first opponents, the Caturiges; and between that town and the Caturigan and Vocontian frontier (Fines) he would have to fight his many actions with the Centrones, Garoceli, and Caturiges. But the Centrones of the Tarentaise, and the Garoceli of the Lower Maurienne, are not likely to have found themselves here: they would have been entirely separated from the Caturiges of Chorges by the Vocontii, Tricorii, and Uceni, and by the Cottian Quadiates and Segusini. The same would also be the case if the route from Gap to Grenoble were adopted.

Indeed Messrs. W. and C. seem to be aware of the improbability of their route, even after they have placed inaccurately the tribes who opposed Cæsar. The Caturiges, they say (p. 21), "occupied Briançon and the valley of the Durance as far as Embrun." But Briançon is given by Ptolemy to the Segusi(a)ni, meaning perhaps to the Segusini as the chief and representative of the Cottian tribes. It is also certain that the Caturiges must have possessed the town of Caturiges (*Chorges*), and thus have lived below the frontier town of Embrun, instead of above. The Centrones, it is rightly stated by Messrs. W. and C. in their text, lived in the Tarentaise; an opinion to which they do not strictly adhere in their map, where they extend them into the Maurienne up to the Mont Cenis. The Garoceli, they say (p. 21), "must have inhabited the valleys in the vicinity of Mont Cenis and the Upper part of the Maurienne;" but they place them in their map, more correctly, in the Lower Maurienne, though erroneously giving there to the Centrones what they had given in their text to the Garoceli. Yet even these arrangements do not appear to have removed in their minds the difficulty of the route which they have chosen. "It is not improbable," they say, "that Cæsar may have sent part of his army through the country of the Centrones in the first instance, as also another division through that of the Garoceli" (p. 21), the main body passing by the Mont Genèyre (p. 22). This would be a strange hypothesis for any one to make, but above all for those who speak of the pass of the Mont Cenis as certainly not a Roman road (p. 172). And how could each one of three passes be the 'proximum iter per Alpes'?

I have now only to shew how Centrones, Garoceli, and Caturiges, may have opposed Cæsar on the route of the Mont Cenis. As to the first two tribes there is no difficulty; for Cæsar would approach nearer the Centrones by this line, than he could do by any other route from Ocelum. He also passes through *Sanctus Joannes Garocellius*. The only difficulty results from the mention of the Caturiges, and this may be plausibly if not satisfactorily explained. If Strabo is right in placing Centrones, Catoriges, Veragri, and Nantuates, in the mountains above the Salassi, then we have Caturiges probably in the Upper Maurienne, and certainly near the Centrones. There is also another reason for finding Caturiges on the road from the Mont Cenis to Grenoble. On one route in the Peutingerian Table occurs Catorigomagus = Caturiges (*Chorges*), and on another a station called *Catorissium*, not improbably indicating the town of the *Catorisses* or *Caturiges*. It is quite indifferent to my argument whether this station be placed, as I should place it, at Villarodin in the Upper Maurienne; or, as is usually done, at Bourg d' Oysans, or Vizille, or at some intermediate place in the lower valley of the Romanche. In the first case, Cæsar would meet with the Caturiges before he met with the Garoceli; in the latter, afterwards, when he had crossed the Col de la Croix de Fer, and entered the valley of the Olle, a tributary of the Lower Romanche.

Let me recapitulate the leading points in the argument. Cæsar is to start from Ocelum on the Dora, 99 M. P. from Embrun, and therefore 28 from Susa: he is to take the shortest road (to Lyons): he is to pass through Grenoble, and to reach the Vocontian frontier in seven days from Ocelum: and he is to be opposed, between the Cottian and Vocontian frontiers, by Centrones, Garoceli, and Caturiges. These conditions seem to me to leave no route for him but that of the Mont Cenis and the Col de la Croix de Fer, and so on to Grenoble; either (as is most likely) by the Col de la Coche, or else by the valleys of the Olle and Romanche.

I am glad to see that Mr. Law no longer extends the Centrones into the Maurienne, as he did in the map which formed part of his criticism on my first work. But he assigns to the Caturiges of Chorges and Embrun, like Messrs. W. and C., Briançon and the country of the Cottian Quadiates or Quariates; and also removes the Garoceli from the Maurienne to the valley of the Clusone. May I be allowed, in the interests of geography and humanity, as well as in those of the Mont Cenis, to object decidedly to Mr. Law's annihilating every one of the original Cottian tribes, and assigning lands to such other tribes as he pleases in the territories thus placed at his disposal? If the position of the *Garoceli*, who were hostile to Cæsar, is to be defined by any *Ocelum* at all, it should be by one beyond the limits of the Cottian Land, such as *Usseglio* or *Esseillon;* and not by *Ussolo*, *Exilles*, or *Usseaux*, which last Mr. Law makes to serve also as the *Ocelum* from which Cæsar started. It is doubtful to whom *Usseglio* and the valleys of the northern Stura belonged, but probably, I think, to the Salassi. In addition to instances of the old Celtic name for high places found in Gaul and Spain, our own island gives us the ancient *Ux-ellum*, *Uxella*, and *Ocelum* or *Ocellum* Promontorium, as well as the modern *Ochill* Mountains and *Ochiltree*, 'Higham, Hochheim, Hauteville.' *Uchaf* and *Isaf*,

'Upper' and 'Lower,' are common additions to Welsh names.

The route of Plancus from Grenoble to the Verdon (B.C. 43).

There is no difficulty about the march of Plancus, of which an account is given in Cicero, *Epist. ad Div.*, lib. x., 11, 15, 17, 18, 21, 23.

After Antony's defeat at Mutina, he was eventually obliged to abandon Italy, and crossed the Maritime Alps to Forum Julii (*Fréjus*). At this time there were two Republican armies in Gaul. One, under Lepidus, lay at Forum Voconii, which Plancus makes to be 24 M. P. from Forum Julii, but the Antonine Itinerary, probably more correctly, only 12; so that Forum Voconii would be near the modern *Le Muy*.

The other Republican army was under Plancus. When he heard that Antony was besieging Decimus Brutus in Mutina, he had crossed the Rhone into the country of the Allobroges with the intention of passing the Alps and relieving Brutus; but, hearing of the defeat of Antony, he remained among the Allobroges.

Lepidus now summoned Plancus to join him at Forum Voconii; and Plancus, in pursuance of his instructions, throws a bridge (at Grenoble) over the Isère, "flumine maximo, quod in finibus est Allobrogum," and starts with the expectation of reaching Forum Voconii in eight days, leaving his bridge guarded for the use of Decimus Brutus, whose arrival from Italy was expected.

The distance from Grenoble to Forum Voconii (*Le Muy*) is as follows :

	M. P.	
Grenoble (*Cularo*)		
Gap (*Vapincum*) .	68	(101 kilomètres)
Sisteron (*Segustero*) .	33	(Ant. Itin.: modern dist. 32)
Riez (*Reii*) . .	48	(71 kilomètres)
Antes	32	Peut. Tab.: modern dist. 47)
Forum Voconii (*Le Muy*)	19	
	200	

This distance Plancus expected to perform in eight days, which would require him to march at the rate of 25 M. P. daily. Cæsar, as we have seen, fighting the greater part of his way, only accomplished 20. It is obvious that no longer road, such as that by Valence and Die, can be chosen for Plancus, as in such a case he could not have expected to reach Forum Voconii from Cularo in eight days.

Meanwhile, Lepidus, being about to revolt from the Republic, and join Antony, countermanded his directions for the advance of Plancus. Yet Plancus, although suspecting Lepidus, did not discontinue his march, but continued to advance, and eventually encamped at a distance of 40 M. P. from Antony and Lepidus, both at Forum Voconii. Plancus describes himself as encamped with a river in his front, and the "Vocontii sub manu, per quorum loca fideliter illi pateret iter."

As Reii was 49 M. P. from Forum Voconii, the river behind which Plancus encamped would have been the Verdon. He lay in the country of the Albiœci, whom Strabo makes to border on the Vocontii, through whose country Plancus had, as he says, a safe retreat (to Cularo). It seems to be inferred from this, that the route from Grenoble through Gap and Sisteron lay in the Vocontian territory, which amply confirms the eastern extension which I have given to the Vocontii.

On the 29th of May the suspected defection of Lepidus to Antony was completed, and the two generals marched on the same day to encounter Plancus, who heard of their approach when they were 20 M. P. off, and therefore after they had marched 40 – 20, or 20 M. P. Plancus now begins his retreat, in all probability on the 30th of May ; and terminates it on the 4th of June, by crossing the Isère, breaking down his bridge, and waiting to be joined by Decimus Brutus at " Cularo in finibus Allobrogum," which is the suburb of Grenoble, called St. Laurent, on the north side of the Isère. The 160 M. P. from the Verdon to Grenoble would thus have been accomplished by Plancus in six days. He retreated at the rate of 26 or 27 M. P. daily.

CHAPTER VIII.

CONSIDERATION OF TWO ROUTES IN THE PEUTINGERIAN TABLE—AND
OF A PASSAGE IN AMMIANUS MARCELLINUS.

Two routes are found in the Peutingerian Table between the route of the Little St. Bernard leading from Aosta to Vienne, and the route of the Mont Genèvre leading from Susa to Arles.   Both these two intermediate routes are made to branch off from the route to Arles on the summit of the *Alpis Cottia* or Mont Genèvre; so that the road from Susa into Gaul is thus made to split into three distinct roads on the summit of that mountain.   Of course there must be some error here; and when we come to consider the two intermediate routes further, we shall see that they are represented very erroneously.   For, if we take the distances marked on them to be correct (and we are without the means of suggesting any emendations, although it must be admitted that the Peutingerian distances frequently are erroneous), Vienne, to which both of the routes lead, would lie only 85 M. P. from the Mont Genèvre, and Luc only 46; which is exactly the modern distance from Luc to Gap, a city about 70 M. P. from the summit of the Mont Genèvre.

As a first step to the correction of the Table, let us try to determine what the lower route marked there from the Genèvre to Vienne really was.   It begins thus:

I

In Alpe Cottia				M. P.
Gerainas .	.	.	.	XIIII
Geminas .	.	.	.	XIIII
Luco	.	.	.	XVIII

and then proceeds along the ordinary road by Die and Valence to Vienne.

D' Anville, not being acquainted with the country, made this route proceed from Briançon, and cross a difficult pass more than 10,000 feet high into the Val Godemard, fixing the station of Gerainæ at *Jarain*, and tracing the route thence to *Mens*, considered to be Geminæ, and so on to Luc. This supposed route deserves mention, on account of the high character of its proposer as a geographer, though the probability of such an hypothesis can hardly now be admitted for a moment. I subjoin a comparison of the Peutingerian distances with the *straight* distances between D' Anville's stations : the travelling distances between them would of necessity be very considerably greater :

	Peut. dists. M. P.	St. dists. M. P.
In Alpe Cottia (*Briançon*)		
Gerainas (*Jarain*) . . .	XIIII	XXXII
Geminas (*Mens*)	XIIII	XVII
Luco (*Luc*)	XVIII	XXII

Another hypothesis for this Peutingerian route is given in his Ancient Atlas by Spruner, who makes a certain approximation to the truth. According to him, the route to Luc branched off from the route to Arles, not on the Genèvre, but at Chorges. His Gerainæ would apparently be *St. Laurent*, and he holds with D' Anville in fixing Geminæ at *Mens*. I compare Spruner's route with that of the Table, as I have previously compared D' Anville's.

	Peut. dists. M. P.	St. dists. M. P.
In Alpe Cottia (*Chorges*)		
Gerainas (*St. Laurent*) . . .	XIIII	XII
Geminas (*Mens*)	XIIII	XXIII
Luco (*Luc*)	XVIII	XXII

I may suggest the following as a third hypothesis. For the positions of Les Gareins and Luz, see the map.

	Peut. dists. M. P.	St. dists. M. P.
In Alpe Cottia (*Gap*)		
Gerainas (*Les Gareins*) . .	XIIII	XII
Geminas (*Luz*)	XIIII	X
Luco (*Luc*)	XVIII	XIIII

This looks plausible; but I believe that the nature of the country which the route would have to traverse between Gap and Luz would render such a line highly improbable. The resemblance between the names of *Gerainæ* and *Les Gareins* does not, I think, count for much, for such names are common. In addition to the *Jarain* of D'Anville, there is a place called *La Gareine* near *Les Gareins*, and another called *Gareines* to the south of Chorges. I derive these names from Raymond's map. It is possible that this rugged limestone district was called *Gerainæ*, and that the name may be equivalent to τραχῶνες, Τραχωνῖτις, and connected with the Welsh *garw*, *geirw*, 'rough.' There is a place called *Aspres* near Jarain, and two more called *Aspres* and *Aspremont* between Gap and Luc.

My own solution of the difficulty which the Peutingerian route presents is this: it was identical, or very nearly so, with the regular route between Gap and Luc, which would otherwise be wanting in the

Table. The following is the comparison of the ancient routes and the modern road between Luc and Gap; a road rather shorter than that of the Antonine Itinerary, because it avoids the elbow made at Mons Seleucus (*La Bâtie Mont Saléon*), and takes the more direct line through Aspres.

ANT. ITIN.		JERUS. ITIN.		PEUT. TAB.		MODERN ROAD.		
	M. P.	Luco	M. P.	Luco	M. P.	Luc	kilom.	M. P.
Luco		Vologatis	IX					
		Cambono	VIII			La Baume........	23	XVI
				Geminas XVIII				
Monte Seleuci	XXVI	Monte Seleuco	VIII			Aspres	13	IX
		Daviano	VIII			Veynes	8	V
				Gerainas XIIII				
		Ad Fines	XII					
Vapineo.. XXIIII		Vapineo (XI., } read ...... }	VI¹	{In Alpe Cottia, { read Vapineo XIIII		Gap	24	XVI
	L		LI		XLVI			XLVI

I believe the Peutingerian route should be explained in this manner, and that at any rate it must be considered as having branched off from the route to Arles, not on the summit of the Genèvre, but at Gap, 69 or 70 M. P. in measured distance from that mountain. I now proceed to consider the second of the two doubtful routes in the Peutingerian Table.

This route is commonly supposed to be that which leads over the Col du Lautaret from Briançon to Grenoble, and so on to Vienne. The chief reason for this supposition is, that there are two stations, *Culabo* and *Morginnum*, placed 14 M. P. apart, on the route, and that these may be probably identified with Grenoble, anciently called *Cularo*, and with *Moirans* (on the river *Morge*), 15 M. P. from Grenoble. Against this supposition there is the objection, that the Peutingerian route makes Vienne only 85 M. P. from the Genèvre, and that the distance from Briançon to Vienne by the modern road over the Lautaret is about 140 M. P.

Or change the previous XII into VII.

Again : if we identify Culabo with Grenoble, and Morginnum with Moirans, Vienne ought, according to the Table, to be 29 M. P. from Moirans, the true distance being 65 kilomètres = 44 M. P. But this objection may be easily obviated. As we have been already obliged to unfasten these Peutingerian routes at one end, the Mont Genèvre, and are compelled merely to assume that they branched off somewhere, as at Briançon or Gap, from the great road over that mountain; so now we must make a similar assumption, for the second of the Peutingerian routes, with respect to its other end at Vienne. This second of the two Peutingerian routes lying between the road to Arles and the road from the Little St. Bernard to Vienne, would have reached, at the distance of 29 M. P. from Morginnum, not Vienne, but the route from the Little St. Bernard to Vienne. Only one station, Turecionicum, is placed on the Table between Morginnum and Vigenna (*Vienne*); and the other station or stations requisite to complete the route must be supplied from the route between Vienne and the Little St. Bernard, as all the stations requisite to complete the Peutingerian route from Luc to the Mont Genèvre, namely Gap, Chorges, Embrun, Rama, and Briançon, have to be supplied from the route between Arles and the Genèvre.

Proceeding on this principle, we shall find that the last Peutingerian route from the Genèvre to Vienne would be identical with one of three roads : the road from Gap (69 M. P. from the Alpis Cottia) over the Col de St. Guigues to Grenoble and Bourgoin (*Bergusia*, 20 M. P. from Vienne), which was the route of Plancus ; the road from Briançon (6 M. P. from the Alpis Cottia) to Grenoble and Bourgoin (20 M. P. from

Vienne); or the route from Susa (30 M. P. from the Alpis Cottia) over the Little Mont Cenis to Maltaverne (at or near *Mantala*, 80 M. P. from Vienne), which was the route of Hannibal and Artemidorus. I will now compare these three routes with the route of the Table, giving the supposed positions of the stations on the route of the Lautaret as they are usually given, and identifying the stations on the route from Gap to Vienne, which has never, I think, been suggested as the Peutingerian route, in the manner most favourable to such an hypothesis. As the distances on the route of the Little Mont Cenis are derived from my own estimates, I will add an argument in support of their general correctness. The distance from Chambéry (Lemincum) to Susa, by the high road over the Great Mont Cenis, is given at $67\frac{1}{2}$ Piedmontese miles = $112\frac{1}{2}$ M. P., leaving nearly $112 - 16 = 96$ M. P. between Mantala and Segusio. By taking the Little Mont Cenis instead of the high road over the Great Mont Cenis, about 7 M. P. are saved, which would leave 89 M. P. from Susa to Maltaverne. St. Jean de Maurienne is placed at a distance of 38 Piedmontese miles = 63 M. P. from Susa by the high road, and would therefore be 56 M. P. from Susa by the Little Mont Cenis.

The following is the comparison of the Peutingerian route with the three roads in question :

1st road.

PEUT. TAB.		M. P.	COL DE ST. GUIGUES.	kilom.	M. P.
In Alpe Cottia (Vapinco)		M. P.	Gap	kilom.	M. P.
Stabatione	. . .	VIII	Brutinel . . .	13	VIIII
Durotinco	. . .	VII	Guinguette de Boyer .	10	VII
Mellosedo	. . .	X	Corps . . .	14	X
Catorissium	. .	V	*Quet* . . .	9	VI
Culabone	. . .	XII	Grenoble (*Cularo*) .	55	XXXVII
Morginno	. . .	XIIII	*Moirans* . . .	22	XV
Turecionico .	.	XIIII	Longe Chenal . .	22	XV
Vigenna (Bergusia)	.	XV	Bourgoin . . .	23	XVI
		LXXXV			CXV

All agrees here with the exception of the distance between Catorissium and Culabo, where we have 12 M. P. instead of 37. But I may just notice that the Geographer of Ravenna, who is, however, of scarcely any authority, inserts a *Fines* between *Catorissium* and *Culabo*, and reads: "Juxta præfatam civitatem Canduribagus (= Catorigomagus, *Chorges*) est civitas quæ dicitur Sanatione, Durotingo, Metrozelon, *Cantourisa, Fines, Curarone*, Maurogena, Urdonno, Luco, Bococilon (= Dea Vocontiorum, *Die*), Auguston." But *Fines* seems the explanation of *Culabo*, which would be identical with the Gaelic *culaobh*, 'tergum.'[1] If a station Fines were to be inserted between Catorissium and Culabo, it might be used as evidence in the following manner:

	M. P.		kilom.	M. P.
Catorissium (Fines *Catorigum* et Tricoriorum)	v	Quet .	9	VI
[Fines (Tricoriorum et Vocontiorum) .	xxv]	Vizille .	37	xxv
Culabone (in finibus Allobrogum) . .	xii	Grenoble	18	xii

2nd road.

PEUT. TAB.				COL DU LAUTARET.			
In Alpe Cottia (Brigantione)			M. P.	Briançon		kilom.	M. P.
Stabatione .	.	.	VIII	Le Lauzet .	. .	21	XIIII
Durotinco .	.	.	VII	La Grave .	. .	17	XII
Mellosedo .	.	.	x	Bourg d' Oysans	.	31	XXI
Catorissium	.	.	v	Vizille .	. .	30	XX
Culabone .	.	.	xii	Grenoble (*Cularo*)	.	18	XII
Morginno .	.	.	XIIII	*Moirans* .	. .	22	XV
Turecionico	.	.	XIIII	Longe Chenal	. .	22	XV
Vigenna (Bergusia)	.		XV	Bourgoin .	. .	23	XVI
			LXXXV				CXXV

---

[1] A word still preserved in the *Col de la Cula* and the *Col de Coulaon* near the Viso.

3rd road.

PEUT. TAB.			LITTLE MONT CENIS.		
In Alpe Cottia(Segusione)		M.P.	Susa		M.P.
Stabatione .	.	VIII	La Ferrière .	.	VIII
Durotinco .	.	VII	On the summit	.	VIII
Mellosedo .	.	X	Bramans .	.	X
Catorissium	.	V	Villarodin .	.	V
Culabone[1] .	.	XII	Orelle .	.	XIII
Morginno[2] .	.	XIIII	St. Jean de *Maurienne*		XIIII
Turecionico	.	XIIII	La Chapelle	.	XV
Vigenna (Mantala)	.	XV	Maltaverne	.	XVI
		———			———
		LXXXV			LXXXIX

I leave the reader to form his own conclusion from these comparisons. My own preference is for the route of the Little Mont Cenis, though I admit that a good deal may be said for the route of the Col de St. Guigues. The route of the Lautaret I think the least probable of the three. The distances do not fit; the name Catorissium seems to require that the Caturiges of Chorges should be extended to Vizille; and we have no record, as we have in the case of the two other passes, of any ancient passage by the Lautaret.

On a passage in Ammianus Marcellinus.

This author wrote in the latter part of the fourth century of our era. In the 10th chapter of the 15th book of his history, he gives the following account of the passage of the Cottian Alps:

" *In his Alpibus Cottiis, quarum initium a Segusione est oppido, praecelsum erigitur jugum, nulli fere sine discrimine*

---

[1] Fines Catorissium (Catorigum) et Medullorum.

[2] Written by the Geographer of Ravenna *Maurogena*. It appears from the Appendix to the Works of Gregory of Tours that the ancient name of St. Jean de Maurienne, in the Latin of the Merovingian age, was *Maurigenna, Morigenna, Maurienna,* or *Morienna.* We learn from the same authority that it derived the name of St. Jean from a supposed relic of St. John the Baptist, which was preserved there.

penetrabile. Est enim e Galliis venientibus prona humilitate devexum, pendentium saxorum altrinsecus visu terribile, præsertim verno tempore: cum liquente gelu, nivibusque solutis flatu calidiore ventorum, per diruptas utrinque angustias, et lacunas pruinarum congerie latebrosas, descendentes cunctantibus plantis homines et jumenta procidunt et carpenta; idque remedium ad arcendum exitium repertum est solum, quod pleraque vehicula vastis funibus illigata, pone cohibente virorum vel boum nisu valido, vix gressu reptante paullo tutius devolvuntur. Et hæc, ut diximus, anni verno contingunt. Hieme vero humus crustata frigoribus, et tanquam levigata, ideoque labilis, incessum præcipitantem impellit, et patulæ valles per spatia plana glacie perfidæ vorant nonnunquam transeuntes. Ob quæ locorum callidi eminentes ligneos stilos per cautiora loca defigunt, ut eorum series viatorem ducat innoxium: qui si nivibus operti latuerint, montanis defluentibus rivis eversi, agrestibus præviis difficile pervaduntur. A summitate autem hujus Italici clivi, planities adusque stationem nomine Martis (*Oulx*) per septem extenditur millia : et hinc alia celsitudo erectior, ægreque superabilis, at Matronæ porrigitur verticem (*Mont Genèvre*), cujus vocabulum casus fœminæ nobilis dedit.[1] Unde declive quidem iter, sed expeditius, adusque castellum Virgantiam (*Briançon*) patet."

The latter part of this passage is easily understood; and the plain, said to be seven M. P. in length, is the level valley which extends for nearly that distance from Oulx towards Susa.   Yet the rest of the description, which I have marked by italics, would not be verified in the narrow valley or ravine, which extends from the eastern extremity of the *planities* to Susa; but it would be an accurate picture of the descent from the Mont Cenis, while *from the summit of the Italian declivity* of the Cenis another plain of about seven M. P. in length extends to the Col of the Little

---

[1] As in the case of the *Plan des Dames* on the Bonhomme.

Mont Cenis.   I am inclined to think that Ammianus
had received accounts both of the Mont Cenis and the
Mont Genèvre, and confounded the plateau of the
Mont Cenis with the level valley below Oulx, so as to
make two passes into one.   The error in the Peutingerian Table is partly of the same nature, and may be
owing to a similar misconception.   The constructor
of that table seems to have confounded the *Alpes
Cottiæ* with the *Alpis Cottia*, and thus to have made
all the Cottian routes meet on the Genèvre.   For the
Mons Gaura, though not in the Cottian Land, may be
considered as belonging to that division of the Alps
which is called the 'Cottian,' rather than to the
'Graian' or 'Maritime' Alps; and the route by the
Genèvre and the *Mons Gaura* is, in point of fact,
called in the Antonine Itinerary, *Iter a Mediolano
per Alpes Cottias Viennam.*

APPENDIX.

1.—*On the word 'Leucopetron.'*

EXCEPT in the account of Hannibal's march through the Alps, there is only one passage in Polybius where this word occurs, and here it seems nearly equivalent to our English word *crag*. I have given below at length the narrative of Polybius where *Leucopetron* is thus found for the second time, as the account helps to shew the nature of mountain warfare, and to illustrate the story of the battle fought by Hannibal, when he eventually encamped "near a certain strong *Leucopetron*," to protect the march of his army. In my Treatise on Hannibal's Passage of the Alps I have identified this *Leucopetron* with the Rock of Baune, a crag about a mile long, and perhaps 500 feet high, which completely bars the valley near St. Michel in the Maurienne. The Rock of Baune, and the Rock of Esseillon (*ante*, p. 42, note) which strikes the eye of every traveller, are the two great λευκόπετρα ὀχυρά of that valley.

The passage in Polybius which I now subjoin is found in lib. x. cap. 29, 30, and relates to an expedition of King Antiochus. It runs thus:

"Antiochus therefore determined to march into Hyrcania. But when he came to Tagæ, and learned from the inhabitants the difficult nature of the country that he would have to pass through till he reached the summit of Mount Labus which declines towards Hyrcania, and also the numbers of the Barbarians who beset in places the difficult passes (ταῖς δυσχωρίαις αὐτοῦ), he determined to divide his unencumbered men (τὸ τῶν εὐζώνων πλῆθος), and to distribute them under their leaders, so as to be ready to act upon any emergency. In like manner also he arranged the pioneers (τοὺς λειτουργούς), who were to accompany the unencumbered men, and prepare any place which these had taken possession of for the passage of the phalangites and the baggage-animals. Having thus resolved, he gave the command of the van to Diogenes, placing under him archers and slingers, and such of the mountaineers as were able to hurl darts and stones: these fought without order, but were of the greatest service in the difficult passes, by always being ready for the attack individually whenever the time and place required it. Next in order were placed about two thousand Cretans with bucklers, under the command of Polyxenidas the Rhodian. Last came those armed with breastplates and with shields, who were commanded by Nicomedes the Coan and Nicolaus the Ætolian.

As they proceeded on their march, the ruggedness and narrowness of the passes were found to be much greater than the king had anticipated. For the whole length of the ascent (τῆς ἀναβάσεως) was about three hundred stadia; and for the greater part of this distance they were obliged to make their way through a deep ravine traversed by a mountain-torrent, and where the passage was impeded by trees and by many rocks which had fallen into it from the precipices above. These impediments were also much increased by the Barbarians: for they made a series of barricades by felling the trees, and piled up quantities of great stones, while they themselves remained on the watch, having occupied all along the gorge the commanding eminences, where they might likewise be in safety. In this manner, had they not committed an oversight, they would have forced Antiochus to abandon an attempt which he would have been entirely unable to accomplish: for they made their preparations and occupied their posts on this supposition, that their enemies would be absolutely obliged to effect their ascent through the ravine itself. Yet they did not perceive, on the other hand, that it was indeed impossible for the phalanx and the baggage to pass in any other manner than they had anticipated, for these were unable to gain the slopes of the mountains; whereas an ascent among the crags themselves (ἡ δι' αὐτῶν τῶν λευκοπέτρων ἀναβολή) was not impracticable for the light-armed and unencumbered. And thus, when the first posts of the Barbarians were reached by the troops of Diogenes, who were making their ascent outside the ravine (i. e. on the slopes above, not in or near the bed of the torrent), the aspect of affairs was changed. For, as they saw at once from the nature of the case what was to be done in such circumstances, they struck obliquely up the mountains and thus got above their enemies, severely galling them by incessant showers of darts and close volleys of stones, and harassing them especially with their slings from a distance. When they had thus driven the Barbarians away and taken possession of their posts, the pioneers had time to clear the obstacles in the passage entirely away, and to smooth the road in safety: and this was soon done on account of their great number. In this manner, as the slingers, the archers, and the dartmen, advanced along the heights dispersedly, but gathering together at times and seizing the commanding positions; and as the men with bucklers guarded the march, and advanced in regular order and march through the ravine; the barbarians did not stay to hold their ground, but all, abandoning their positions, collected on the summit of the pass."

The circumstances of Antiochus appear to have been more favourable than those of Hannibal. Antiochus anticipated an attack on his van, and made preparations to resist it accordingly. Hannibal expected an attack on his rear, was prepared to resist it, and repelled it. But he was also attacked on his flank (and I think unexpectedly) in the van; as Antiochus would have been, had he not previously dislodged the Barbarians. Both would probably have dislodged the Barbarians on the heights in a similar manner, but with a rather different result. Antiochus outflanked the Barbarians in their posts, getting above them; and thus obliged them to retreat up the valley, and not higher up the side of the mountain where the contest took place. Hannibal seems to have got in like manner above the posts of the Barbarians, but after they had left them and retreated higher up the mountain on the side of the valley, instead of up the valley itself. Thus the subsequent operations were different. The light troops of Antiochus proceeded up the valley, along the mountains, continually dislodging the Barbarians, and thus protecting their own army in the valley below. Hannibal, having the Barbarians partly above him on his flank, and partly behind him hanging on his rear, encamped, instead of marching, in a kind of semi-circle round the *Leucopetron*, kept off in this manner the Barbarians from the more defenceless part of his army, and allowed it to march on ahead. It may be asked, why Hannibal did not advance along the flanks of the mountains, and why the Barbarians did not thus proceed oftener, so as to hover over the Carthaginian army, as it marched on through the valley. The precipitous character of the Alps may have rendered this in general impracticable.

It may be thought that the Rock of Baune is too near the summit of the Little Mont Cenis to mark the limit of Hannibal's progress on the fourth night of his march from the town of the Allobroges (Allevard). For that rock is about 50 Roman miles from Allevard, and hardly 35 from the plateau of the Little Mont Cenis, which would have been gained on the morning of the ninth day. Hannibal would consequently have marched to the Rock at the rate of 13 miles a-day, and from it to the summit of the pass at not more than 8. But several considerations make this difference probable.

1. From the Town to the Rock Hannibal's march was not impeded, but facilitated, by the inhabitants, while from the Rock to the summit he was subject to repeated attacks.

2. Up to the Rock of Baune the road lies nearly always in an open valley; but from the Rock to the summit the old path runs for the most part on the mountain-sides, in consequence of the valley becoming a ravine except where the basins of Modane and Bramans occur.

3. Hannibal's track would most nearly resemble an Alpine footpath of the present day: that is to say, it would be comparatively broad, well made, and well defined, in the lower part of the valley, but would deteriorate in every respect the farther he advanced towards the summit, where the snow had most likely begun to fall, and thus to present an additional impediment to the advance of the army.

4. After fighting on the fourth day, and either marching or protecting the march during the whole of the fourth night, little progress would probably have been made by the Carthaginians on the fifth day.

Hannibal's itinerary during the fifteen days of his march from Allevard to Avigliana might be thus conjecturally given:

DAY		M. P.
1. Allevard to Chamoux	. . .	$14\frac{1}{3}$
2. Chamoux to La Chapelle	. . .	15
3. La Chapelle to St. Jean de Maurienne	.	$14\frac{1}{3}$
4. St. Jean to Rock of Baune	. . .	$7^{[1]}$
5. Rock of Baune to Orelle	. . .	7
6. Orelle to Modane	. . .	$9\frac{1}{3}$
7. Modane to Bramans	. . .	8
8. Bramans to beginning of plain on summit	.	$7\frac{1}{2}$
9. On the summit	. . .	$3^{[2]}$
10. Halt on summit continued	. .	
11. Summit (middle of plain) to La Ferrière	.	$7^{[3]}$
12. Halt to make the path	. . .	

[1] This allows the battle to commence about mid-day.

[2] Reckoning to the middle of the plain, which is above six Roman miles in length from the Col of the Little Mont Cenis to La Grande Croix.

[3] Descent stopped about mid-day by the destruction of the path.

DAY				M. P.
13. La Ferrière to Venaus	.	.	.	6[1]
14. Venaus to near San Giorio .		.	.	13
15. Near San Giorio to Avigliana.		.	.	14

For these last two stages the march would have lain through an open valley. Deducting the four days of halting, namely, the two on the summit, and the two between the middle of the 11th and 13th days, the average length of a day's Alpine march would have been about 11½ M. P. Polybius makes it about 13. All but experienced pedestrians are liable to overrate distances walked in mountains.

2.— *On the Approach to the Alps by the left bank of the Isère.*

It has been attempted to retaliate upon this route the objections brought against the line of approach which the Bernardine advocates select for Hannibal, and which makes him, instead of following the Isère from its confluence with the Rhone, prefer to make a circuit over mountains which Polybius describes as almost inaccessible, in order to come back to the Isère again. With this view Messrs. W. and C. affirm (p. 178):

1. "There is no road whatever on the left bank of the Isère, and such is the nature of the country, that there never could have existed any route in that direction."

And again, p. 157:

2. "M. Letronne forgets that Polybius positively states the army to have marched these 100 miles through a plain country, ἐν τοῖς ἐπιπέδοις, c. 50. Now, such a country, between Valence and Grenoble, it is quite impossible to find."

And finally, p. 51:

3. "I (we) apprehend that infinitely greater difficulty (than in crossing the Chartreuse mountains) would have been experienced in marching up its (the Isère's) southern bank, as the defiles in the neighbourhood of

---

[1] Path completed for the elephants in the afternoon, after an enforced halt during three days; and the whole army again reunited, the cavalry and baggage-animals having passed before.

Grenoble are so narrow, and the mountains of Dauphiné plunge so perpendicularly into the river, that it would be quite impossible to carry cavalry and elephants by that line."

I shall first answer the first and third of these statements.

As a carriage-road now exists along the left bank of the Isère between Valence and Grenoble, it follows that it cannot be true that "there is no road whatever on the left bank of the Isère," or that "such is the nature of the country, that there never could have existed any route in that direction." This carriage-road is, however, in its present state, of late construction; though there always appears, as far as is known, to have been a road here. I shall indeed be able to prove that there was a road practicable for armies along the left bank of the Isère as far back as three centuries ago. This will appear from the account given by M. Pilot of the local religious wars in his History of Grenoble (pp. 148—187), from which I have derived the statements which follow. As I have put the names of the places on the left bank of the Isère in italics, they may be at once recognised, and referred to upon the map.

April 25, 1562. The lieutenant-general of Dauphiné, Pardaillan, is murdered at *Valence* by the Huguenots, under their leader, Des Adrets. (*Valence* appears throughout these wars to have been the Huguenot head-quarters.)

May 11. Des Adrets enters *Grenoble*, and carries off cannon thence to *Valence*.

The Catholic leader, Maugiron, takes possession of *Grenoble*, and leaves the Baron of Sassenage in possession of it.

Des Adrets takes St. Marcellin, and enters *Grenoble*, June 26. He returns to Lower (*i. e.* West) Dauphiné, leaving Lacoche at *Grenoble*.

Lacoche is besieged at *Grenoble* by the Baron of Sassenage. A body of 700 foot and 80 horse march under Furmeyer to relieve him. They arrive at *Noyarey*. It appears from Videl's Life of Lesdiguières (p. 18, ed. 1650) that Furmeyer started from *Valence*:

"Furmeyer, qu'un nouveau dessein avoit amené près de *Valence*..... s'avance à *Sassenage*, &c."

Furmeyer defeats the Baron on the *Drac*, and relieves *Grenoble*.

Dec. The Huguenots, with Des Adrets, assemble the Provincial States at Montélimar. A general impost for the war is decreed, and it is resolved to establish a council for the province at *Valence*.

Crussol succeeds Des Adrets in the chief command of the Huguenots.

Feb. 28, 1563. The Catholics under Maugiron besiege *Grenoble*. Crussol marches to its relief.

Maugiron hears that Crussol has arrived at *St. Quentin*. He raises the siege, March 3. Crussol enters *Grenoble*.

March 19. General peace. Crussol convokes at *Valence* a council for the 20th of April.

1566. The Catholics under Gordes in possession of *Grenoble*.

Nov. 13. Gordes takes Vienne. He then attacks St. Marcellin, but retires at the approach of Mouvans and Crussol.

Crussol intends to march upon *Grenoble*, but, having no siege-artillery, only advances as far as *St. Quentin*, which he takes.

Jan. 1, 1567. The Catholics attack *St. Quentin*, which surrenders. It is retaken by the Huguenots on the 17th or 18th of February.

March 23. General peace. Gordes dismantles *St. Quentin*.

March 1580. The Catholic general, Maugiron, besieges Moirans. The Huguenot Lesdiguières marches to relieve it. He is about to cross the Isère at *Veurey*, when he hears of the fall of Moirans. He nevertheless forces the Catholic army to retire from the country, which he lays waste. He then returns by the way he came (*retourna sur ses pas*), withdrawing the detachments he had posted at Tullins, *St. Quentin*, and *Iseron*, in order to protect his retreat.

Another passage, from Videl's *Life of Lesdiguières* (p. 78), may be added:

1580. Le Duc (de Mayenne) voyant Tallard avitaillé, part de *Valence*, une nuict; remonte le long de l'Isère, du costé de *Beauvoir*, petite ville, foible de murailles et de garnison: et..... la fait investir par quatre mille hommes.

It will be seen from these passages that we have abundant proof of the existence of a road by which an army could pass, three centuries ago, along the left bank of the Isère from Valence to Grenoble. We trace it from *Valence* to *Beauvoir* (28 miles); and thence from *Iseron* (3) through *St. Quentin* (13), *Veurey* (5), *Noyarey* (3), and *Sassenage* (4), to *Grenoble* (4). This may be a sufficient answer to objections 1 and 3. I now proceed to meet objection 2, "that it is impossible to find between Valence and Grenoble a country which might be described as *plain, ἐπίπεδα*." The only difficulty in this matter is to find an account of the country sufficiently particular to notice the fact: but fortunately such an account does exist.

K

There has been published by M. Antonin Macé of Grenoble
an interesting work on Dauphiné, containing a very full description of his native country.[1] It is a translation of part of
a History of the Allobroges by one Aymar du Rivail, who
died about the year 1560. He was probably a native of
St. Marcellin, and certainly studied at Romans; and his book
shews him to speak from personal knowledge as to the nature
of the country in question. He says (p. 180):

"Dans la *plaine* des Voconces qui touche à l'Isère on trouve Saint-
Nazaire, célèbre par un pont solide et étroit sur la Bourne; Saint Jean;
Pont-en-Royans; Saint Just, remarquable par une abbaye construite par
le dauphin Humbert; Beauvoir, maison considérable des dauphins, comme
l'étendue de ses ruines suffit pour le prouver. A peu de distance de là,
les dauphins possédaient et se réservaient pour la chasse la belle forêt
de Claye. On trouve ensuite Iseron, Cognin, Armieu, Saint-Quentin et
Sassenage. Au-dessus de cette *plaine* on monte dans les montagnes des
Voconces, dont les trois premières sont appelées Autrans, Méaudre et
Lans, du nom des villages qu'on y trouve."

It thus appears that the country on the left bank of the
Isère between St. Nazaire and Grenoble may be described
as a plain.[2] As to the part which lies between Valence and
St. Nazaire, I doubt whether any one would deny its claim
to be so called. Instead therefore of "mountains plunging
perpendicularly into the Isère," we find that there is actually
a plain, though it is a narrow one, along the river-side, with
a number of towns and villages; and so far from a road being
non-existent and impossible, it appears that there has always
been one, as far as can be known. With respect to the part
of the Grésivaudan which lies above Grenoble I need say

[1] M. Macé, in an appendix relating to Hannibal's passage of the Alps,
notices the objection I have just been considering against the supposition of the
march along the left bank of the Isère to Grenoble. He says in conclusion:
"Cette objection si formidable, tirée d'une connaissance superficielle des lieux,
tombe d'elle-même quand on a un peu plus sérieusement étudié les localités."
I might perhaps have rested my case upon this testimony of a native of the
country; but the historical evidence of M. Pilot seemed less open to cavil.

[2] I may refer those who are unacquainted with the country to Mr. Allom's
'France Illustrated (I. 39, 72: II. 29).' It will be at once perceptible that the
left bank of the Isère is a plain, though, like the cultivation in the Maurienne
(*ante*, p. 40), it entirely eluded the sight of Messrs. W. and C., when they visited
the Alps, in emulation of Polybius, γνώσεως ἕνεκα καὶ θέας.

nothing, for Messrs. W. and C. have described it (p. 158) as "a valley so rich, and so broad and magnificent, that if Hannibal had once arrived in it, he could never have abandoned it." I do not however perceive the necessity of this last conclusion, nor yet of what follows: "so that, if his original intention had been to march along the Isère, it is also clear that it was equally his intention to go by the Little St. Bernard."

We have evidence of the existence of an ancient road between Grenoble and Aiguebelle nearly in the line that I have marked out for Hannibal to the entrance of the Maurienne. Albanis de Beaumont, in his *Alpes Grecques et Cottiennes* (II. 595), speaks of La Rochette, once a considerable town, as lying on a Roman road from Aiguebelle to Vienne; and Grillet (s. v. *Montmayeur*) is yet more precise: "J'oubliai de dire que sur le coteau où sont situées les tours de Montmayeur, existait une voie Romaine qui conduisait de Maurienne à Grenoble. Au mois d'Avril de l'an 1684, on en découvrit des vestiges très-considérables, lorsqu'on fut obligé de la réparer, occasion du mariage de Victor-Amé II. avec Anne-Marie, fille de Philippe Duc d'Orléans: toute la cour de Turin, qui était venue recevoir la princesse aux frontières du Dauphiné, traversa l'ancienne voie Romaine de Montmayeur pour se rendre à Aiguebelle."

No real objection to the route along the left bank of the Isère as the line of the Carthaginian march is derived from the fact, that Hannibal, for special reasons, entered the 'Island,' the district enclosed by the Rhone, the Isère, and the Chartreuse mountains. For, after the transactions in the Island are concluded, the march is resumed from the confluence of the Rhone and Isère (see my "summaries," *ante*, pp. 21, 22), the point from which the 800 stadia to the commencement of the Alpine ascent are reckoned in any case. The route whose length Polybius measures from New Carthage to the edge of the Italian plain, and which he makes Hannibal to follow, is the actual road or pathway itself, without reference to any divergences from it. Thus, from the Ebro to the Pyrenees (Emporium), Polybius measures the length of Hannibal's march by the length of the coast road,

1600 stadia (III. 39). But it is not likely that the Carthaginians never diverged from it, for we find from the narrative
(III. 35) that Hannibal overthrew on his march the Ilergetes,
the Bargusii, the Ærenosii, and the Andosini, taking many
of their cities, and completely subduing them. Military
history would supply many similar instances. Hannibal's
road need not have *entered* the Island, though he did so with
some of his forces.

Those who take Hannibal through the Island and over
the Mont du Chat make strange confusion with the Allobroges.
According to Polybius, the people of the Island, whom he
leaves unnamed but who may be spoken of as the 'Islanders,'
were friendly to Hannibal and guarded his rear against the
Allobroges while he was in the level country. According to
Livy, the Islanders were Allobroges, and protected Hannibal
against a people whose name is not given. Messrs. W. and
C. unite these irreconcilable accounts, and make the Allobroges
to be both the friends and enemies of Hannibal. Thus the
chief of the Island becomes "the prince of the Allobroges,"
and only protects the Carthaginians "while they are marching
through his territories" (p. 155, note). Yet the Islanders,
after having guarded Hannibal's rear against the Allobroges,
return to their own country (εἰς τὴν οἰκείαν ἀπηλλάγησαν).
It is clear from the whole narrative that the Allobroges of
Polybius did not live in the Island, even though Messrs. W.
and C. argue (p. 177): "If it (the Island) were not then
occupied by the Allobroges, who were no small and obscure
tribe whose territory could with difficulty be traced, we have
a right to be told by what other Gallic clan it was held."
This right is disputable; but the question might probably be
answered, had Dion Cassius given us the name of the people
who were expelled from Vienne by the Allobroges (XLVI. 50).
And if the Allobroges of Hannibal be deprived of the Island,
but allowed to possess the north-western half of Savoy, with
Geneva, the Bugey, the Chartreuse mountains, and the Vale
of Grésivaudan, they would still hold a territory making a
sufficient figure on the map. It would be about 100 miles in
length, and 50 in mean breadth.

3.— *On the Route across the Plateau of the Little Mont Cenis.*

I will first explain from what source my plan of the plateau of the Mont Cenis has been obtained.

It is derived from a model of the Mont Cenis, exhibited in the French Department at South Kensington in 1862, and of which I procured a photograph from the exhibitor. The model itself, as I afterwards found, would have been constructed from a *plan nivelé* of the Mont Cenis, one sheet of which is in the British Museum. This *plan nivelé* seems to have been made under Napoleon I., for in it the artificial cut for the river Cenise to the west of La Grande Croix, which was excavated in 1814, does not appear. I have, however, inserted it. Parallels of altitude, at distances of 20 *mètres*, or 65.6 English feet, were given on the model, in addition to the heights of several particular points. The height of the pass of the Great Mont Cenis, for instance, was given at 2099 mètres = 6885 feet, which is about 100 feet higher than the most usual modern estimate. The *Guide à Suse et au passage du Grand Mont Cenis* (Susa, 1830) gives it at 2100.51 mètres.

By the aid of this plan we may trace Hannibal completely across the plateau. Within a short distance of its western extremity he would arrive at the *Col*, or highest point of the passage. This *Col* lies between the parallels of 2180 and 2200 mètres, and may thus be taken at 2190 mètres = 7183 feet, of elevation. The path now lies for about $3\frac{1}{2}$ miles over the plateau of the Little Mont Cenis, till it reaches, near some scattered buildings called *Les Rivers*, the parallel of 2000 mètres, or 6560 feet. Here it is about 200 feet above the lake, and has descended about 600 in the course of $3\frac{1}{2}$ miles. Between *Les Rivers* and *La Grande Croix*, which is the point for which the path has to make, a range of heights intervenes, extending nearly southward from the lake for about 2 miles, and divided into the hills called *La Montaia, Le Crain, La Montagne du Beet,* and *La Hauteur du Combet.*

The highest of these, the *Montagne du Beet*, has 2120.61 mètres = 6956 feet of elevation, and is therefore about 600 feet above the lake, and rather more than 200 below the *Col* of the Little Mont Cenis. Between this range of hills and the mountains intervenes a small valley called (at least in part) *La Combe*, and through this lies the shortest path to *La Grande Croix*. At the distance of about $1\frac{1}{2}$ miles from *Les Rivers* it crosses the range of hills by a depression between the *Montagne du Beet* and the *Hauteur du Combet*. The elevation of this *Col* is given in my photograph at 2027 mètres, but in the *Plan Nivelé* (which is to be followed) at 2037.14 mètres = 6682 feet. The path has thus ascended for about 120 feet in the $1\frac{1}{2}$ miles from *Les Rivers*. Another mile, with a descent of about 470 feet, brings the traveller to *La Grande Croix* on the edge of the plateau of the Great Mont Cenis, and at the commencement of the abrupt descent into Italy.

Southward from the depression, just noticed, in the hilly range, the long ridge of the *Hauteur du Combet* extends for nearly three-quarters of a mile, till its southern extremity, rising 1000 feet above the plain of St. Nicholas, forms part of the range of cliffs which bear up the plateau of the Mont Cenis. It is from this *Hauteur du Combet*, "promontorio quodam, unde longe ac late prospectus erat" (Livy), that the plains of Italy and the Apennines are to be seen.[1] And there is no difficulty in reaching its summit from the Little Mont Cenis. From the depression in the range of hills (6682 feet) a walk of a quarter-of-a-mile, with an ascent of 6827 − 6682, or of about 150 feet, will lead to its northern summit, and to the " prospect of Italy" (Polybius); though the plains and the Apennines are better seen from its southern summit (6901 feet), nearly half-a-mile further on, and 75 feet higher.

Considering that in the case of Hannibal about 35,000 men would be encamped on the plateau for two days, there

---

[1] I think it is the lowest point on the plateau from which they are visible, but I cannot pronounce with certainty against the *Montagne du Télégraphe* (6639 feet), which forms the southern extremity of the plateau of the Great Mont Cenis. My experience was not gained in very favourable weather.

is no improbability in supposing that some of them may have reached the *Hauteur du Combet* in that time. But yet it is very possible that the army as a body, who would have encamped for the most part on the plateau of the Little Mont Cenis, between the *Col* and the lake, may have been ignorant, during the first day of their halt on the summit of the mountain, that Italy could be seen. And the possibility of this ignorance seems to me, from the account of Polybius, to be almost as essential a point as that the view of Italy should be attainable. For it was on the second day of their halt that Hannibal, finding the prospect of Italy (ἐνάργεια τῆς ᾽Ιταλίας: cf. iii. 111) to be the only thing that could raise the spirits of his dejected followers, *pointed out to them the plains of the Po, and indicated to them the position of Rome.* I find little or no difficulty in this latter expression. "Behind those mountains lies Rome," Hannibal might have said to his soldiers, pointing to the chain of the Apennines, which rose at a distance of 100 miles from their point of view. This view of Italy would have been to the Carthaginians what the sight of the Euxine was to the Greeks in the retreat of the Ten Thousand. A partly similar ἐνάργεια τῆς ᾽Ιταλίας is described by Alison in his account of Napoleon's first Italian campaign, where the march of the French westward from Savona and Monte Notte is related, until they arrived on the crest of the Monte Zemolo:

"From thence the eye could discover the immense and fertile plains of Piedmont. The Po, the Tanaro, the Stura, and a multitude of smaller streams, were descried (?) in the distance at the foot of the mountains; beyond them the blue plains of Italy bounded the horizon;"—not so: the Alps bound the horizon, and the Po and Stura are *in* the plain, which shews itself towards the west and north-west;—"while a glittering semicircle of snow and ice, of a prodigious elevation, seemed to inclose within its mighty walls the promised land. A sublime spectacle met the troops when they arrived on this elevated point; and the soldiers, exhausted with fatigue, and overwhelmed by the grandeur of the sight, paused and gazed on the plains beneath. Those gigantic barriers, which nature had rendered so formidable, and on which art had lavished its treasures, had fallen as if by enchantment. 'Hannibal,' said Napoleon, fixing his eyes on the mountains, 'forced the Alps, but we have turned them.'" Having followed the steps of Napoleon as well as those of Hannibal, I venture to point out where the description of our eloquent historian of the French Revolution is inaccurate.

The pass of the Monte Zemolo, which is situated between the valleys of the Tanaro and the Bormida, is probably about 2500 feet high. Besides a view of the Mediterranean and the Eastern Riviera, which are seen nearly to the E. over the Col de Cadibona (1600 feet) leading down to Savona, the Monte Zemolo commands a prospect of the Alpine chain for a length of nearly 200 miles, as the mountains rise either from the plain on the W. and N.W., or above the Montferrat hills which extend northward from Monte Zemolo to the Po over a space about 50 miles in length. In the centre of this semicircle of Alps may be discerned the gap which forms the pass of the Mont Cenis, though partly intercepted by the lateral ridge which stands to the S. of the valley of Susa. Napoleon might almost have seen the spot from which Hannibal and the Carthaginians looked down upon Italy two thousand years before.

THE END.

CAMBRIDGE:—PRINTED BY JONATHAN PALMER.

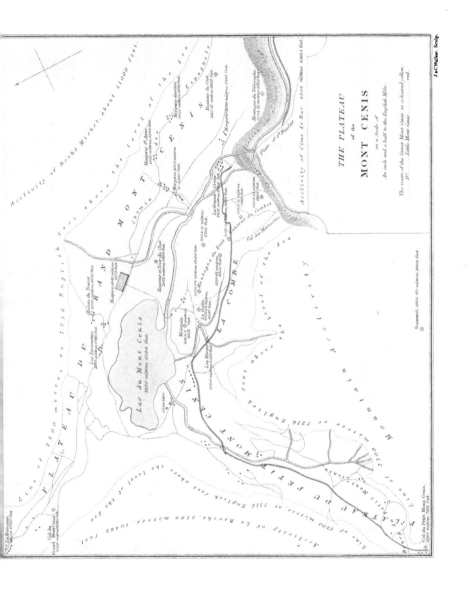

The material originally positioned here is too large for reproduction in this reissue. A PDF can be downloaded from the web address given on page iv of this book, by clicking on 'Resources Available'.

For EU product safety concerns, contact us at Calle de José Abascal, 56–1°,
28003 Madrid, Spain or eugpsr@cambridge.org.

www.ingramcontent.com/pod-product-compliance
Ingram Content Group UK Ltd.
Pitfield, Milton Keynes, MK11 3LW, UK
UKHW012339130625
459647UK00009B/396